Sacha Pignon

21 DAYS TO LEARN embroidery

× daily practice ×

× step-by-step instructions ×

× 16 projects ×

21 Days to Learn Embroidery

First published in the United States in 2025 by Stash Books, an imprint of C&T Publishing, Inc., P.O. Box 1456, Lafayette, CA 94549

This edition of "*21 jours pour apprendre à broder*" first published in France by Éditions Marie Claire in 2023 is published by arrangement with Marie Claire.

PUBLISHER: Amy Barrett-Daffin

CREATIVE DIRECTOR: Gailen Runge

SENIOR EDITOR: Roxane Cerda

ENGLISH LANGUAGE COVER DESIGNER AND LAYOUT ARTIST: April Mostek

ENGLISH TRANSLATION: Kristy Darling Finder

PRODUCTION COORDINATORS: Casey Dukes and Zinnia Heinzmann

DIRECTOR OF EDITING AND REVISIONS: Catherine Zelvelder

DESIGNS, TEXT, AND STEP-BY-STEP PHOTOGRAPHY: Sacha Pignon

STAGED PHOTOGRAPHY: Fabrice Besse, stylist Sonia Roy

GRAPHIC DESIGN AND LAYOUT: Compos Juliot

COVER: Claire Morel Fatio

ISBN: 978-1-64403-619-8

Printed in China

10 9 8 7 6 5 4 3 2 1

DMC
HAPPY

CONTENTS

Herbarium

You hold in your hands a book that will introduce you to the marvelous world of embroidery. Welcome! Let yourself be guided, step by step, to learn and master this ancient yet ever-evolving artform.

This method will allow you to explore the myriad possibilities offered by embroidery, with a wide range of materials including beads, sequins, raffia, ribbons, and even paint!

Together we will encounter all the basics that will allow you to have beautiful technique and—even more importantly—to unite embroidery with your own imagination and achieve the independence of an embroiderer endowed with the true soul of an artist.

Over the course of these 21 days, you will learn various tips for embroidering your clothes, creating decorative objects, and crafting gifts for your loved ones.

Within these pages, I'm offering you the thread of my passion and I hope this journey together will bring you joy. Why not work through these projects with a friend, your little brother, your downstairs neighbor, or a favorite co-worker?

I'm sure that soon you will not be able to let a day go by without embroidering.

Turn the page and have fun!

Sacha Pignon

D·M·C
HAPPY
CHENILLE
D·M·C
HAPPY
CHENILLE
D·M·C
HAPPY
CHENILLE

WHAT A WONDERFUL DAY

to leisurely plan FOR THE DAYS AHEAD!

GATHER AND PREPARE YOUR MATERIALS

It's shopping time! Today you're going to review everything you'll need to get started with embroidery. Get ready to dig through drawers, maybe visit your neighbor or great-aunt to collect various needles or some old tablecloths. To make life a little easier, you can always head to your local craft or fabric store, or check out a few websites.

MUST-HAVES FOR YOUR EMBROIDERY TOOLBOX

Everything to start off right...

- ❑ Needles (Bohin or DMC)
- ❑ Needle threader
- ❑ Thimbles
- ❑ Pins
- ❑ Scissors
- ❑ Pens or other marking tools
- ❑ Measuring tape or ruler
- ❑ Transfer paper or stabilizer
- ❑ Embroidery hoop or frame
- ❑ Clamp
- ❑ Iron

and everything you'll choose specifically for each project.

- ❑ Thread (floss, yarn, raffia...)
- ❑ Fabric
- ❑ Clothes or base of your choice ("Ground")
- ❑ Sewing thread, if needed

❶ *Needles*

Choosing the right needle is key to your comfort. I recommend purchasing needles from DMC, Bohin, or John James, which are all high-quality needles that will make your work easier. For embroidery, we generally use needles that are finer, longer, and have a long eye.

Embroidery needles come in sizes 3 to 12 **(the larger the number, the finer the needle)**. For the projects presented in this book, I recommend you get size 8 or 9 embroidery needles. Naturally, your future projects may require different needles, depending on your fabric and thread.

The thicker your thread, or the more strands you use, the larger your needle—and its eye—will need to be. The needle must also suit the thickness of your fabric, because too fine a needle paired with too thick a fabric will cut into your speed and agility. On the other hand, if you have a **delicate fabric (such as silk)** the eye of your needle must be small to avoid damaging it.

If you want to embroider on **something that cannot handle pointed needles**, use needles with rounded ends or even tapestry needles (for example, if you are embroidering a piece with yarn).

If you want to **embroider on leather**, you'll need to get out your thimble. Then take some thick felt or batting and put it underneath your leather. Take your design and place it on the leather. Then grab a glover needle, which has a triangular point that allows it to pass through dense materials. With your needle, create regular holes to outline your entire design. The felt will help you make regular, well-defined holes. You can then remove your design and embroider your leather using an embroidery needle and the pre-punched holes.

When you embroider with beads—for example, for your sampler or the project on Day 13—you will need to use a "beading" needle, which are numbered 10 to 15. Beading needles are especially long so you can thread several beads at once and their eyes are very narrow to ensure they can pass easily through the beads.

Needle threader

If you're having trouble threading your needle, double-check that you have the right size needle and that it is not damaged, then try turning it over, as the eye of the needle can be wider on one side than the other. If after all this you still can't thread your needle, take advantage of this magical little tool: the needle threader. You can find it in any needle craft shop, it costs practically nothing, and it may spare you some frustration.

Pins

Just like for sewing projects, it's always nice to have a little box of pins on hand for your embroidery projects. They help you properly place your patterns and secure them when it comes time to trace the design onto the fabric. They also let you hold your fabric in place for sewing, if your project includes any sewing steps. A pin can also prove useful to loosen stitches that are too tight, by inserting it under the stitch and gently pulling, or when undoing little snarls that may form on the backside of your embroidery.

These snarls are usually little slipknots. Just slide your pin through the loop and pull on the thread until the loop undoes itself.

Thimbles

When it comes to thimbles, it's up to you. For most projects, this is not an essential tool. However, you will come to realize over the course of this book that a thimble will help you out in some of your creations.

Thimbles come in all different sizes and materials: you will find them in brass, silicon, ceramic, silver, and leather.

Choose one that fits you perfectly: it should stay put if you shake your hand, without ever squeezing your finger too tight. You'll need to break in your thimble so it becomes a natural extension of your hand, so you can wear it all day and even forget it's there.

Different pairs of scissors

Now let's talk about **embroidery scissors**: that indispensable little tool that occupies a place of honor in every embroidery box.

Throughout your creations, you will use them to cut your threads precisely and neatly and to achieve a perfect finish. This will also allow you to more easily thread your needle: naturally, a thread cut by nice sharp scissors will slide through the tiny eye of your needle much more smoothly.

Embroidery scissors are short, between 2 and 6 inches long (6 to15cm), with a very sharp point. Keep in mind, these are scissors for cutting thread only, or else the blade will become dull very quickly. Take care of them!

If you are left-handed, choose a pair of left-handed embroidery scissors.

The second pair of scissors you will need is a larger, more robust pair. Here you have several choices. Ideally, you should have a pair of sewing scissors for cutting fabrics and ribbons (you will also find rotary cutters at fabric stores, which are practical and fast) as well as a pair of paper scissors for cutting water-soluble paper, patterns, etc.

If this seems like too big an investment for now, you can certainly buy one pair of scissors for cutting paper, fabric, and everything else. It won't be quite as comfortable, but it's absolutely acceptable when you're just starting out.

❸ Marking tools

As you will see over the course of the days to come, there are several methods for transferring a design onto a piece of fabric.

The first method consists of using a **marker** or **marking pen** to draw your design directly on the fabric.

There are several types of markers and pens, some come off with water and others with heat.

You can also use FriXion pens from Pilot, which come in a wide array of colors (however, avoid black as it has a tendency to leave yellow traces on the fabric) and can be found in almost every supermarket. These pens are heat-erasable.

If you are embroidering on a **black or particularly dark ground material**, I recommend a **white chalk pencil** or **Bohin's mechanical chalk pencil** which has a very fine tip and allows you to draw easily. If there are still white marks on your work when you've finished your embroidery, take a cotton swab dipped in water (soapy water if needed) and lightly rub the fabric. You can also use Essential White Transfer Paper (C&T Publishing) to easily trace designs onto dark fabric.

❹ Transfer papers and stabilizers

You can also choose to use paper or stabilizer. There are four different types.

- **Carbon paper** comes in several colors; always choose a color that contrasts your fabric. Place the paper between your fabric and your design, pin them all together, then trace over your design with a fine-tipped pen or pencil, pressing quite hard. The pigment of the carbon paper will then be transferred to the fabric.

- The second method involves using an **adhesive stabilizer**, such as Wash-away Stitch Stabilizer (C&T Publishing) or Vlieseline Solufix stabilizer, also called "Magic Paper," which adhere to your fabric and dissolve in water. They're an ideal solution when you're starting out and they're terrific for countering the elasticity of stretch fabrics. However, it's difficult to truly get a sense of the final impression of your embroidery when you can't really see the ground fabric on which it is stitched.

- You can also use **water-soluble stabilizer** which works along the same principle as the other stabilizersr, the only difference being that it is not self-adhesive, so you have to pin it or use a large enough piece to hold it in place with your embroidery hoop.

The last method for reproducing your designs is to use **tracing paper**. For this technique, you need to take your tracing paper, your design, your fabric, an erasable pen (or a marker or chalk), a ball head pin so you don't hurt your fingers, and something soft like a piece of felt or even a cushion. This is the same method you would use for leather embroidery. Start by tracing your design, then position it on your fabric and place a cushion or thick piece of felt beneath it, which will allow you to make regular, well-defined holes. Once your design is perforated, take your tracing paper and pin it to your fabric so that it will not move. Take your marking tool and draw a small dot in each hole you have made. Once you remove the tracing paper, your design will appear as a dotted line.

Measuring tape or ruler

One very simple thing that you probably already have—but which is essential when it comes to embroidery—is a ruler or measuring tape. Used for getting yourself positioned on your fabric, verifying that your placement is aligned, symmetrical, and straight, as well as understanding the scale of your pattern, the ruler is an indispensable element of your embroidery supplies.

Embroidery hoop or frame

Aha! We've finally come to the famous embroidery hoop and frame. These two objects allow you to pull your fabric tight. This is important for several reasons. The first is that it's much more comfortable to embroider when your fabric is not moving. The second reason is that if you fix your hoop or frame to a table using a **clamp**, you will have both hands free and can embroider with one hand above and one hand below your work, saving you a considerable amount of time. The third reason (and the most important!) is that it ensures the regularity of your stitches and a tidy result since the fabric doesn't pull away.

Embroidery hoops allow you to stretch your fabrics quickly and easily and only take up a little space if you need to transport your work. If you're just starting out and you don't know which one to choose, choose a round wooden hoop, between 5 and 7 inches (12 and 17cm).

Know that embroidery hoops come in all varieties to satisfy your creativity: in every size, in wood or plastic, and in all different shapes, including circular, oval, square, and even triangular!

You can also invest in a **seat stand**, which is a stand for your embroidery hoop that slides under your leg and allows you to have both hands free.

Scroll frames are a little harder to transport and to set up, but they offer the best fabric tension and allow you to embroider much larger surfaces. Furthermore, they leave no creases on your fabric, which can happen with embroidery hoops. They also come in several sizes; I recommend starting with a smaller one.

Clamps

The clamp is a very practical object that lets you embroider with both hands while it holds your embroidery hoop or a small frame on your work table. You can find them easily and inexpensively in any hardware store.

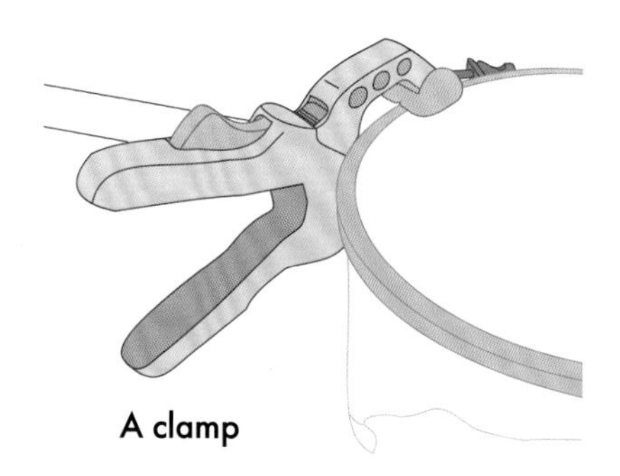
A clamp

Iron

Your iron is a great ally to have for embroidery. You will use it to iron your fabric before you start your project, then to remove any heat-erasable pen marks, and finally to smooth your completed work.

To maintain your iron, descale it using white vinegar and clean the sole plate with baking soda so it doesn't leave any ugly marks on your creations. Bear in mind as well that you can place a piece of fabric or parchment paper between your embroidery and your iron to avoid any accidents.

❺ A cell phone, a window pane, or better yet, a light table

If you choose to transfer your design by drawing on your fabric with a pen or marker, you will need a light source that enables you to see your design through the fabric. You have several options: the simplest is to put your design and your fabric against a window pane with the sun shining through. In the evening, you can use your phone's flashlight to create light beneath your design. The third solution, which is the most comfortable but also requires more materials, is to use a light table.

You can make your own light table. Take two blocks (for example, two thick books), place a light source between them and lay a letter- or A4-sized acrylic sheet on top (which you can find in hardware or art supply stores.) Tada! Your very own light table!

For the rest of your materials, don't forget to take a look at the projects in the coming days!

❻ A nice collection of threads that will arouse your creativity!

Cotton embroidery floss

The best way to stimulate your creativity is to surround yourself with color. Don't hesitate to browse your local craft store and let yourself be swept up in the wide variety of floss, such as **DMC Six-Strand Embroidery Floss**, which comes in 500 colors and is made of 100% cotton! This is also a colorfast thread, so you can machine wash it and it won't discolor from light exposure.

A skein is 8 meters long and has 6 strands. You can divide the skein and embroider with one, two, or as many strands as you'd like. You can also, of course, embroider with several skeins at once.

Pearl Cotton thread, which has similar qualities (find a version that is 100% cotton and colorfast), has a satin finish and more volume than the Six-Strand, so it gives some depth to your embroidery.

It comes in several weights and is non-divisible into strands. It is more solid and thicker than the classic floss.

Silk and rayon thread

If you're looking for a high-quality, solid, and vibrant material, you can also use **silk thread**. This is ideal for a style known as needle painting, which consists of creating entirely embroidered illustrations, as though painted, using a technique of long & short stitches. This is quite an expensive material and must be carefully protected as it has a tendency to pale and deteriorate in sunlight.

As an alternative to natural silk, you can also find rayon. It's an artificial silk, made of a single piece of viscose. It costs considerably less than silk but is difficult to handle. Gently soften it between your fingers before embroidering; this will make your experience much more pleasant.

DMC also offers a nice line of **"Satin Floss"** which mimics natural silk and which we will use over the course of these 21 days.

Metallic threads

If you want to add a little light and sparkle to your embroidery, as we will have the opportunity to do together, you have several options.

DMC Metallic skeins are the most commonly used but they're also difficult to embroider with. Use them for a "sequined" effect or if you want to embroider with a golden thread, for example. It's a thread I don't recommend to beginners because it's inflexible and has a tendency to fray over time from passing through the fabric.

There are, however, some tips to know when it comes to taming this tough thread: first of all, use a short needle with a large eye, then use short lengths of thread, and lastly, the best advice is to combine a metallic thread with cotton embroidery floss to help it slide more easily.

DMC Diamant spools are used for this same reason. These are spools of two-stranded thread (one metallic and one cotton), so the thread is somewhat more flexible and a little easier to embroider with.

DMC Étoile skeins are made of 6 strands 8 meters long, just like the Six-Strand Embroidery Floss. They are a mix of cotton and sparkling threads, so it has a subtler finish than the metallic threads.

This is a thread I really like for adding brightness, and we will use it together because it is flexible, soft, and it slides easily through your fabric. I recommend using short lengths of thread to avoid snarls at the eye of your needle.

Fil à gant (Gloving thread)

Au Chinois brand thread is a waxed linen thread. It is perfect for securely embroidering beads and sequins.

Yarn

You can also embroider with yarn, providing you have the right needle and the right technique. For example, to embroider a sweater, choose a large yarn needle with a rounded tip so as not to damage the stitches of your fabric. For this type of work, I prefer DMC's Tapestry Wool, which comes in skeins, or balls of DMC Natura Just Cotton, which is good quality and does not shrink in the wash.

Chenille

Chenille is an interesting type of thread, with a velvety quality. You can embroider with it using a large needle with either a rounded or pointed tip, depending on your ground fabric. The highest quality chenille is silk chenille, which you can find in a wide range of colors from the brand Au Ver à Soie, but it's a rather expensive material. You can also find it in balls and of synthetic material, which will also have a beautiful appearance once embroidered.

Raffia

Raffia is a nice material you can find in different colors and different qualities. It can be shiny when it's synthetic or matte when it's natural. You can braid it or use individual strands.

For this type of thread, I recommend using a pointed chenille needle. This is a thread we will work with together on Day 16. You can find it in certain hardware stores, gardening centers, and of course in craft stores.

If you want to try out other kinds of threads not listed above, you can certainly draw on the advice given to help you find an appropriate technique for your project. And don't forget that the most important thing is to choose the right needle, **the right ground fabric, and the right type of stitch** (which you can find in your collection of stitches).

❸ Your "ground" – the fabric, clothing, or other material of your choice

Fabric

With fabric, the possibilities are obviously innumerable. In theory, any fabric can be embroidered. If you're just starting out, choose a fabric that won't get you into trouble. Opt for a fabric that holds up well (not too thin, not too thick), no stretch, made of natural materials, and with a tight enough weave that your stitches don't let daylight through your fabric.

For example, choose a cotton fabric. I would favor colorfast fabrics, and prewash them before embroidering to make sure they won't shrink and that they don't fade in the wash.

Evenweave fabrics for counted needlework

For cross stitch projects (or any counted needlework), choose a fabric that has an open and even weave like linen, cotton muslin, or Aida cloth.

Stretch fabric

Stretchy, flexible, shapeless jersey demands the correct preparation, as we will see on Day 8. The techniques explained there will apply to all stretch fabrics.

Felt

You will use felt for finishing your embroidery projects, as we will see on Day 5.

Felt is available in a wide variety of colors and thicknesses. It's pleasant to sew and can be cut without risk of fraying.

❹ Sewing thread, if needed

You will use sewing thread if you're working on projects that require sewing. Buy a spool of thread that matches your embroidered fabric. If you would rather add a more whimsical touch, choose a thread in a contrasting color, particularly a color featured in your embroidery; this will bring harmony and coherence to your final project.

THAT LITTLE EXTRA SOMETHING

The little accessory to have on hand and which won't cost you a cent is a trash receptacle for your thread. Your embroidery workspace may quickly devolve into chaos if you don't have one, and you'll find little bits of thread hanging off all your clothes. To avoid this inconvenience, find an empty jam jar to keep within arm's reach. After a few projects, you'll have a pretty pot of colors to testify to your embroidery work.

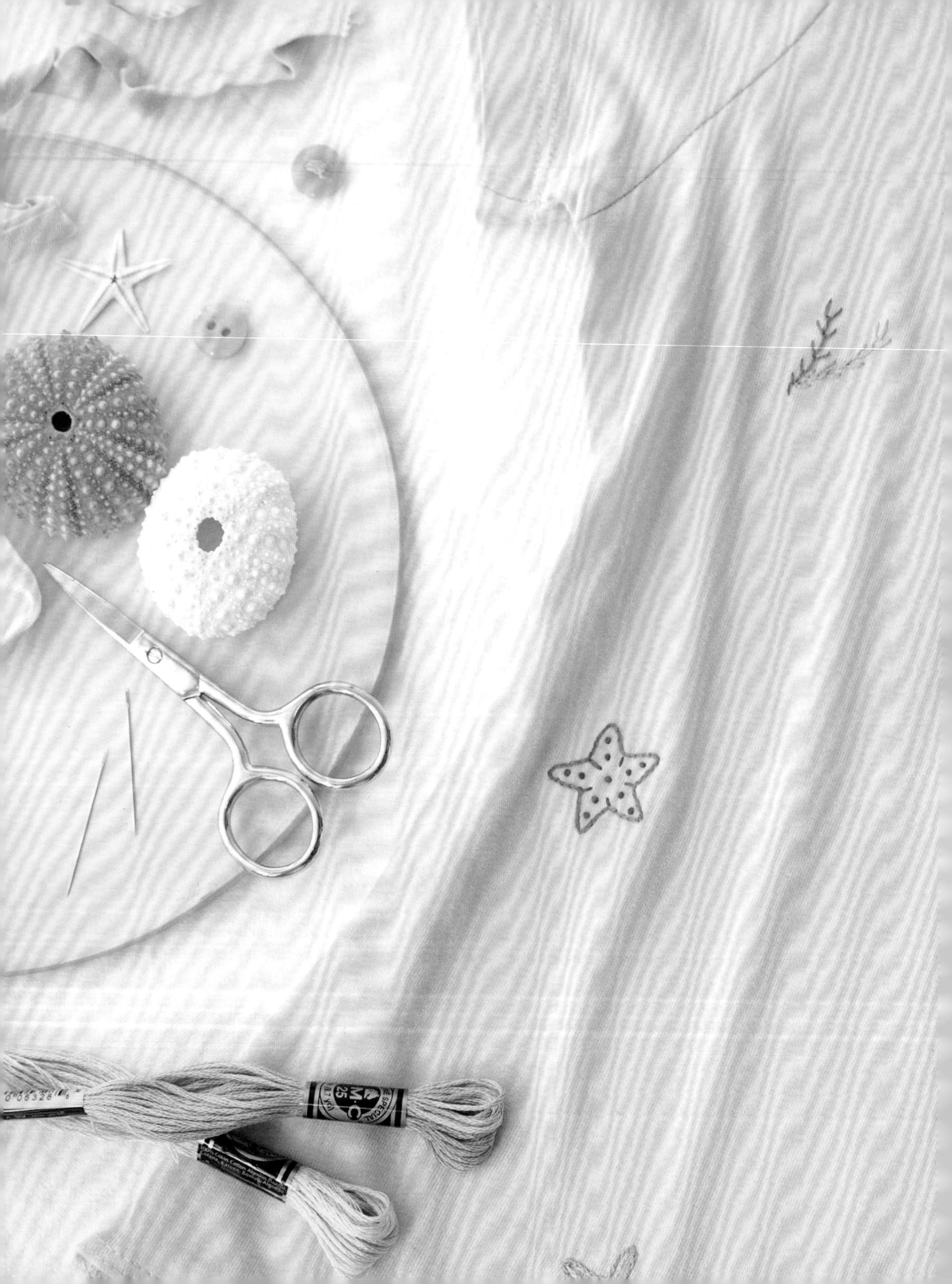

SHALL WE BEGIN?

LEARN TO START YOUR EMBROIDERY PROJECTS

Lesson #2... A very pleasant day: the time has come to arrange your little workspace and complete the preliminaries that will allow you to take your first steps into the world of embroidery.

Get settled in and comfortable. Choose a room that you like, a place where you can be calm and focused. To each their own: a desk or a sofa, all that matters is that it feels right to you.

If possible, have some fresh air; carve out a corner of a balcony, patio, garden, or your favorite café's outdoor seating... The natural light is best for your eyes. Embroidery requires attention to details and a particular concentration of the eyes. Make sure you have the right lighting so you don't wear yourself out.

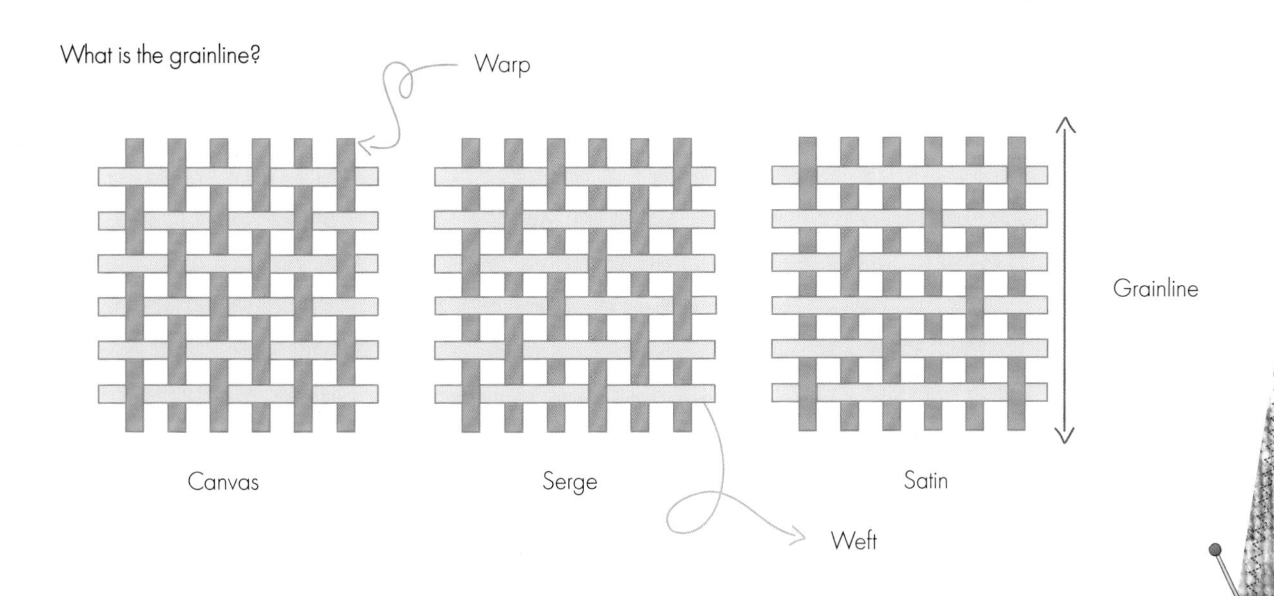

❶ Prepare your fabric

If the fabric is new, send it through a quick wash to avoid any future issues (like shrinking) after you've embroidered your piece. Then—and do not skip this step—give it a quick iron so it will be flat and smooth. Last, cut the fabric square to be placed in your embroidery hoop. To know what size to cut, add 4″ to the diameter of your hoop.

A little technical note

What is the grainline? Fabric is composed of **warp threads** and **weft threads**, and together they form the fabric's **weave**, or how the threads overlap. The fabric's warp is always parallel to the selvage, or finished edge, of the fabric. By working with the grainline (also called the straight or lengthwise grain), you are ensuring that your fabric won't become misshapen later on. (See diagram on the previous page.)

❷ Transfer the design

Now that your fabric is ready, you can transfer your design. Whichever method you choose, always make sure your fabric is immobile during this stage.

If you want to change the size of your design, you can use a scanner, which will enable you to select a percentage of magnification or minimization. Always bear in mind that if you change the size of the design, you may also have to adapt your stitches and how they are used.

Have a look back at the previous day, and you have everything you need to know when it comes to transferring your design.

This mental map will help you see things a little more clearly:

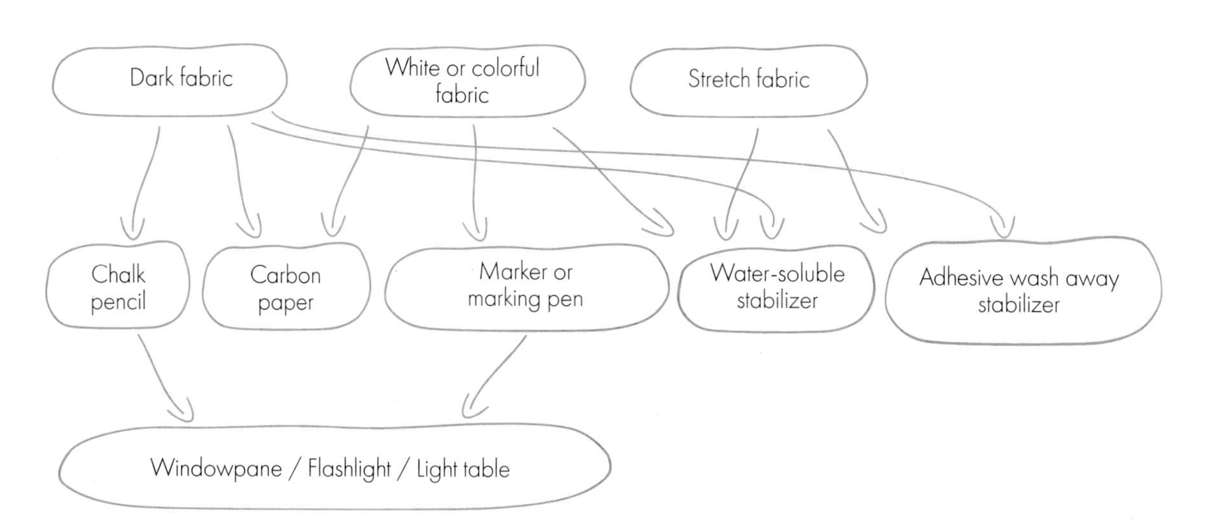

❸ Prepare your embroidery hoop or frame

Once you've prepared your fabric and transferred your design, it's time to set up your embroidery hoop or frame.

If you've chosen to work on a hoop, here's a little basic advice to optimize its use: Wrap the interior circle of the hoop in a cotton ribbon or a strip of fabric. This will reduce slippage and allow for better fabric tension.

All you have to do is loosen the screw, separate the two circles and place your fabric on the smaller of the two circles, making sure your design is centered. Then put the larger circle around the smaller one and tighten the screw so that your fabric is stretched tight.

If you have chosen to work on an **embroidery frame**, you need to mount your fabric straight across the top and bottom strips to ensure equal tension throughout your fabric, pull the fabric tight, then add two ribbons on the outer edges, which you will fix in place using pins. To attach the ribbons, follow the diagram below. Run the ribbon over the wooden bar, then under, then over, etc.

If you're taking a long break away from an embroidery project, take your work out of the embroidery hoop to avoid any crease marks on the fabric.

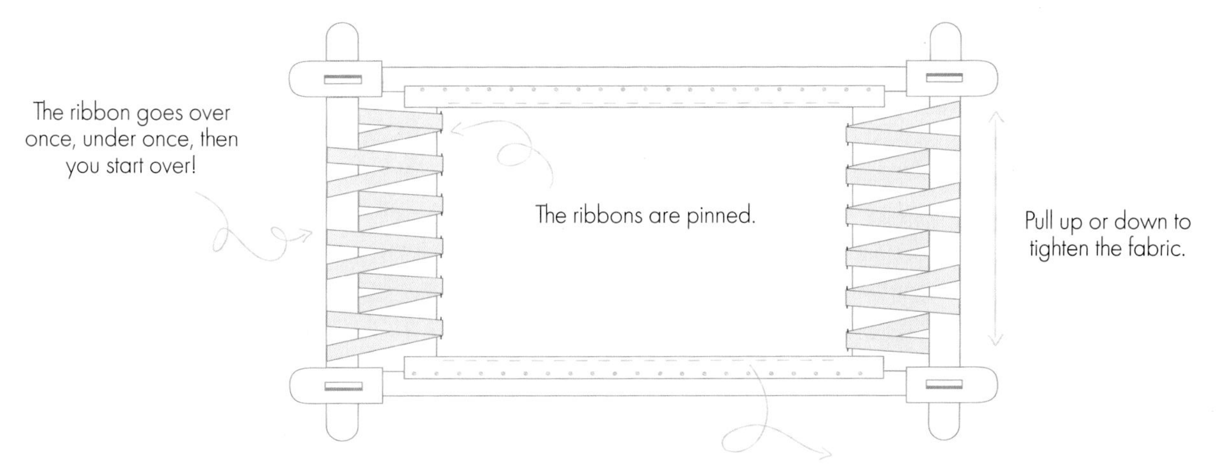

❸ Prepare a length of thread

Take a skein of embroidery floss, whichever color you've chosen and take off the larger band with the reference number (if you need to keep this reference number, roll your skein onto a little piece of paperboard and write the number there), then slide the other band to the middle of the skein. Gently pull on the end of the thread and separate the number of strands you will need. Hold the strand(s) between your fingers until the thread reaches your elbow. With your other hand, slide the other strands back from the ones you will use. This is called stripping the strands. If you are doubling your thread, double this distance; if not, cut the strand(s) you'll be using with your embroidery scissors.

Bear in mind that if you cut too long a length of thread, you increase your risk of making knots on the backside of your hoop. With a little practice, you'll soon be able to cut your thread without thinking through all these steps.

If you still wind up with loops in your thread under your hoop, it's because the thread has become twisted as you've embroidered. In this case, simply let go of your needle and let it dangle. The thread will untwist itself.

Take the strand(s) you have cut, moisten if needed, and thread your needle. If it you can't seem to do it, switch out your needle or use a needle threader.

Once your needle is threaded, pull on the shorter end of the thread so it extends 4" (10cm) beyond your needle, so you don't accidently unthread your needle along the way.

When you begin embroidering, you will go from stitch to stitch using the same length of thread. Carrying the thread from stitch to stitch is often called a "pass." Passes should not be longer than a ½″ (1cm) for several practical reasons: your stitches may become too weak if the pass is too long, your fabric may pucker* when removed from the embroidery hoop as this changes the fabric tension, and lastly, if you're working with a light fabric, you may be able to see these long passes through the fabric. So when it comes to carrying across from one stitch to the next: always ½″, maximum!

*Pucker: make tiny creases and folds

Secure your thread to the fabric

Everything is ready for you to begin your embroidery. Our last subject for today will be how you choose to attach your thread to your fabric.

The three ways of starting your thread:

Attaching a double thread

We will often be embroidering with what we call a double thread, meaning one strand folded into two. It's very nice working with a **double thread** because the thread is fine enough to slide easily through the fabric. The thread holds onto the needle well enough that you don't accidently unthread it, and the final result is really attractive. The color comes out vibrant and the volume of the thread is maintained.

If you are embroidering with an even number of strands, there is another very practical method for starting your work.

To **attach a double thread:** take the strand you've stripped from the skein. Fold the strand in half and thread the two ends of your strand through the eye of the needle.

Poke your needle through from the back side of the fabric. Pull the needle out above the embroidery hoop, holding onto the middle fold of your strand underneath the hoop with your other hand.

Still holding onto the little loop under your embroidery hoop, stick your needle back into your fabric, right next to your previous stitch, so that you will pull the needle through the loop on the reverse of your fabric.

Push the needle back through to the right side of your fabric. You can hide these two little attachment stitches with the first (or last) stitches of your embroidery.

Knots

To attach your thread to the fabric, you can also **knot** it in place.

There are **two ways to make a knot in embroidery.**

- You can make a knot at the cut end of you thread, then insert your needle through the reverse side of your embroidery hoop and pull the needle through. It's an easy solution but not a very secure one. You can use this method for decorative embroidery—projects that won't be handled or washed.
- The second method for knotting your thread is a little more technical but you will embrace it very quickly. Insert your needle through from the reverse side of your fabric, holding 4″ (10cm) of thread with your other hand underneath the embroidery hoop. Poke back through your fabric, right next to your first stitch, and pull the needle through on the reverse. Knot the thread from your needle with the cut end of your thread, then poke the needle through between these two stitches to get back onto the right side of your fabric.

Knots are practical because it's something everyone is used to doing and it's almost instinctive. It is perhaps not the best solution in embroidery because after a few wash cycles, or if they are repeatedly agitated (as on the back of a jacket, for example), knots will eventually come out. So they should be avoided, unless your embroidery will be framed.

The three tiny stitches method

This method is the most classic and the most thorough in embroidery. It works well both for **starting your thread** at the beginning of your work and for **finishing your thread**. Insert your needle into the reverse of your fabric, holding onto ½″ (1 cm) at the end of your thread beneath the embroidery hoop. Pull the needle through on the right side, then make a second stitch very close to the first.

Insert your needle back into the same spot and make the same stitch in reverse, and insert the needle once more so that the third tiny stitch goes through the first two stitches.

Hide these stitches beneath your first or last embroidery stitches. This method is secure and discreet.

❸ The three ways of finishing your thread:

Remember to always leave enough of a tail to finish your thread.

Burying the thread

The first technique we'll look at is primarily used for cross stitching, but you can also use it for any work that will be framed.

Once your thread has only a few inches left at its end, put the needle through to the back side of your embroidery and turn the embroidery hoop over. Then pass the need underneath the last stitches made to hold it in place, or wrap the thread around the last stitches you made.

Knotting

You can also knot your thread to finish, and in this case, I suggest **two methods**.

- Pull your needle through to the back side of your fabric then form a loop as though to make a knot. Once your loop is formed and you have it between your fingers, turn it over. This movement will allow you to then slide it by pulling the end of the thread until your loop is against the fabric. Make two or three knots to really fix the thread in place.
- The second method requires a little extra dexterity but guarantees your knots will always be right against the fabric. Pull your needle through to the back side of the fabric and hold it in your left hand.

Insert your needle in the same spot and pull it through on the right side, making sure to hold a loop on the back side with your left hand.

Insert your needle through the same spot so that the pointed end of the needle is on the reverse side while the eye of the needle remains on the right side. Twist the loop in your left hand twice around the needle then pull the thread through downward, gently sliding the loop so that a knot forms against the fabric.

The three tiny stitches method

You can also finish your thread using the same method of three tiny stitches that we've already discussed. Hide your three tiny finishing stitches under your last embroidery stitch and cut the thread on the reverse side of your work.

Point de chaînette

Point de feston

Point de tige

Point d'arête

Point d'épine

Point d'étoile

Point de noeud

Point de poste

Point de roue

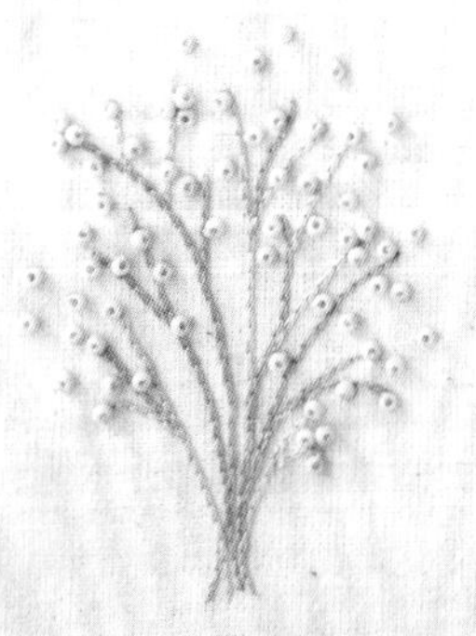

Perles à la puce

Perles au point arrière

Sequins en deux points

A BEAUTIFUL COLLECTION OF STITCHES

to learn your EMBROIDERY ESSENTIALS!

LEARN AND UNDERSTAND THE MOST IMPORTANT EMBROIDERY STITCHES

A collection of stitches, in theory...

The best way to get started in embroidery, to get comfortable using a needle, and to learn how to gauge thread tension is to make a sampler. Today, you will learn the theory and familiarize yourself with all the essential stitches. A sampler is sort of like your little embroidery bible!

Our collection of stitches

1 Line stitches

- Running stitch
- Whipped running stitch
- Back stitch
- Split back stitch
- Couching stitch
- Chain stitch
- Blanket stitch
- Stem stitch

2 Filling stitches

- Cross stitch
- Satin stitch and long & short stitch

3 Decorative stitches

- Fly stitch
- Star stitches
- Feather stitch
- Fishbone stitch
- Lazy daisy

4 Embellishments

- French knots
- Bullion knots
- Woven wheel stitch
- Tuft couching

5 Beading

- Beaded fringes
- Scattered beads
- Back-stitched beads

6 Sequins

- Double-stitched sequins
- Beaded sequins
- Back-stitched sequins
- Overlapping sequins

Line stitches

The first stitches we will dive into will let you create the outlines of your designs.

Running stitch

To make a running stitch, pull the needle through to the right side of your fabric at **A**.

Insert the needle at **B**, then pull it through again at **C**.

Continue making nice even stitches in this way on the surface of your fabric.

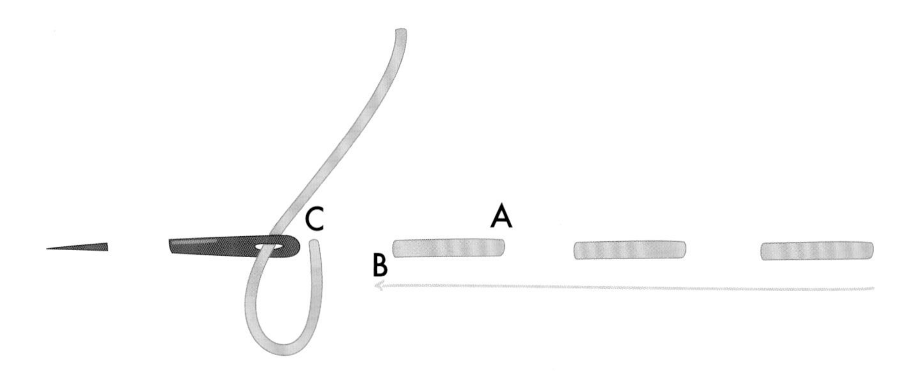

Whipped running stitch

To make the whipped running stitch, begin by embroidering a running stitch.

Prepare a length of contrasting thread then pull it through to the right side of your fabric at **A**, below the first stitch of your line of running stitches. If you would like, you can use a needle with a rounded tip for this second step, so as not to split your running stitch.

Slide your needle through each stitch from top to bottom without sewing into your fabric and without pulling too tight; your thread should remain relaxed and keep its volume.

Pull the needle through to the reverse side of the fabric to finish your line.

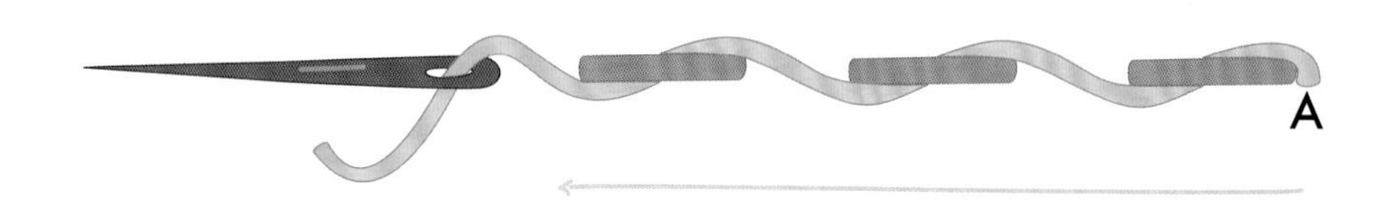

Back stitch

To make a back stitch, pull the needle through to the right side of the fabric at **A**.

Insert the needle a little behind it at **B**, the pull the needle back through at **C**, the same distance from **A** as **B**.

To create a nice line of back stitches, make sure all your stitches are the same length.

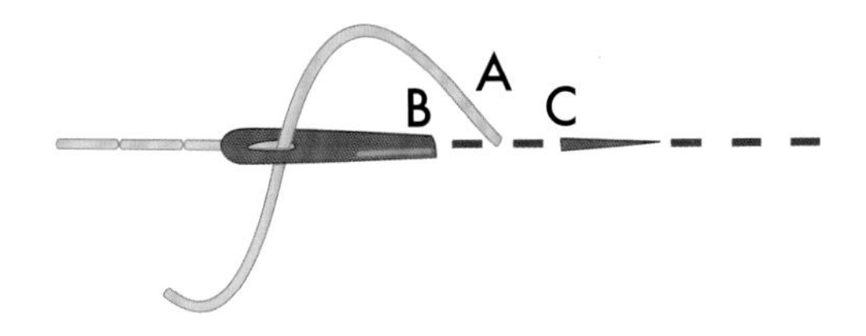

TIP

When you want to make a right angle, finish your line then use a single running stitch to create the right angle, then continue with the back stitch.

Split back stitch

To make a split back stitch, pull the needle through to the right side of the fabric at **A**.

Insert the needle a little behind it at **B** then pull the needle through at **C**.

Insert the needle at **D**, splitting the **AB** stitch you have already made.

Continue your stitching, always splitting the previous stitch.

Couching stitch

To make a couching stitch, begin by preparing the threads to be attached by this stitch and bring them through the fabric at **A**.

Then pull the couching thread through to the right side of the fabric, below the other thread and very near **A**.

Come through the fabric at **B** and insert the needle at **C**. Continue making your little couching stitches in this manner at regular intervals all along your other thread.

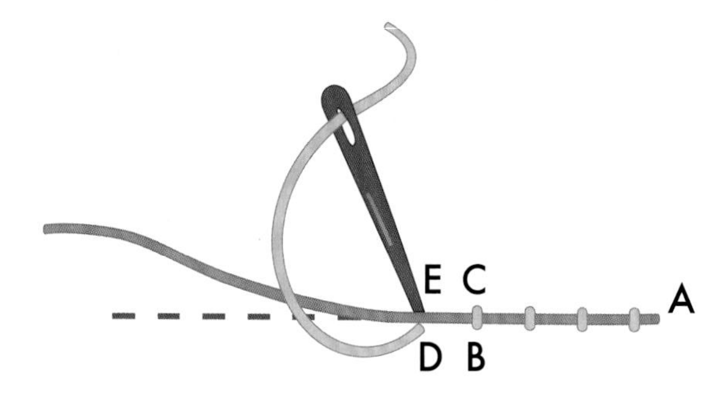

Chain stitch

To make a chain stitch, pull the needle through to the right side of your fabric at **A**.

Reinsert your needle at **A** and pull it out at **B** so that your needle passes over the loop of thread you have made.

Reinsert your needle at **B** and pull it out at **C**, and repeat these steps until your line is complete.

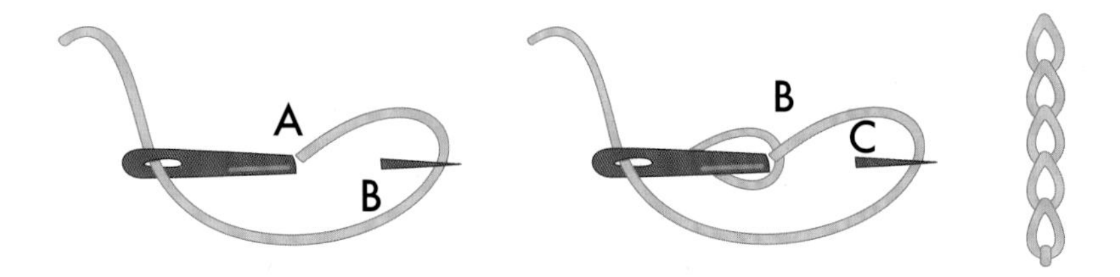

Blanket stitch, as a line or an eyelet

To make a blanket stitch, pull the thread through at **A**, then insert the needle at **B** and pull it out at **C** so that the loop is held under your needle.

Insert the needle at **D** (if you are making an eyelet as in the second diagram, points **D** and **B** will be the same) and pull it through at **E** so that your loop is held under your needle. Repeat these steps until the end of your line or your circle.

Always hold your loop in place with your fingers so that it remains properly oriented.

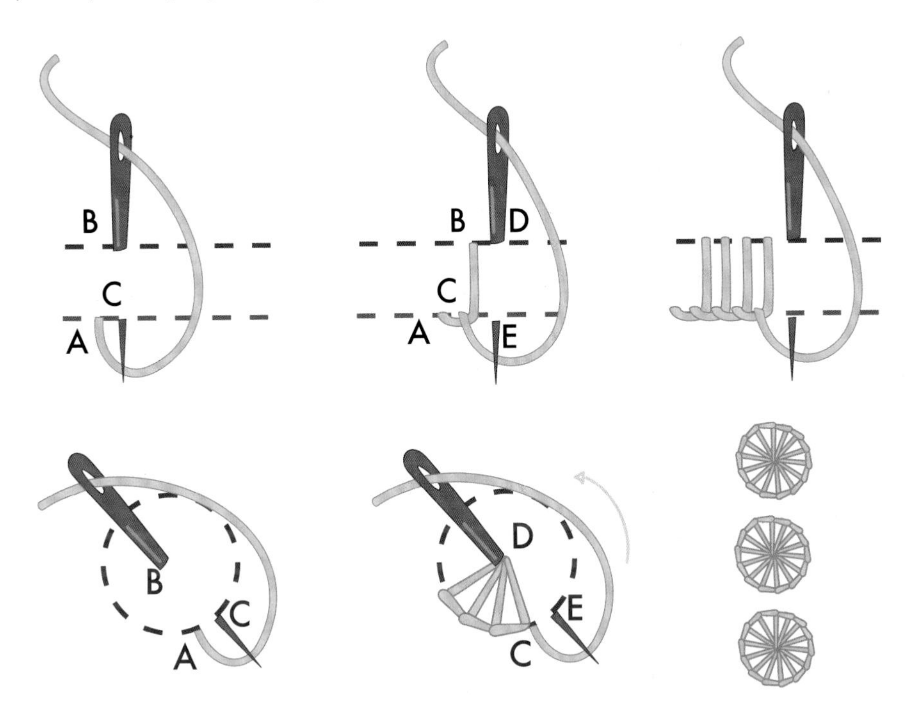

Stem stitch

To make a stem stitch, pull the needle through to the right side of your fabric at **A**.

Insert your needle at **B** and pull it through at **C**, half-way between **A** and **B**, and slightly offset from the **AB** line.

Insert your needle at **D** and repeat these steps. Continue until you have finished your line.

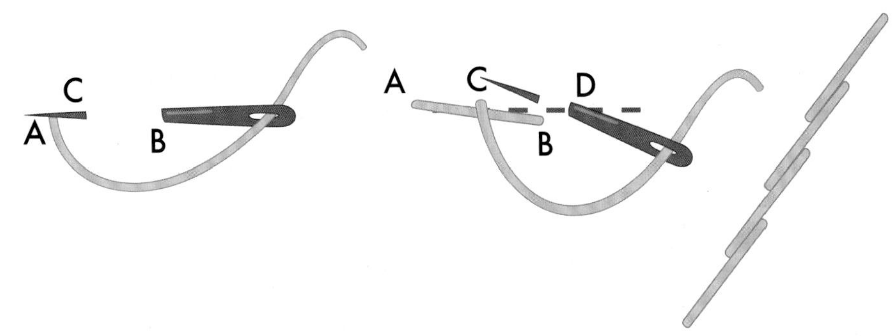

❸ Filling stitches

These stitches enable you to create very pretty patches of color.

Cross stitch

To make a cross stitch, pull your needle through to the right side of the fabric at **A**.

Insert your needle at **B**, pull it out at **C**, insert at **D**, and so on until the end of the row.

Create the second row in the same way as the first, completing your crosses: pull the needle through at **A**, insert at **B**, and so on.

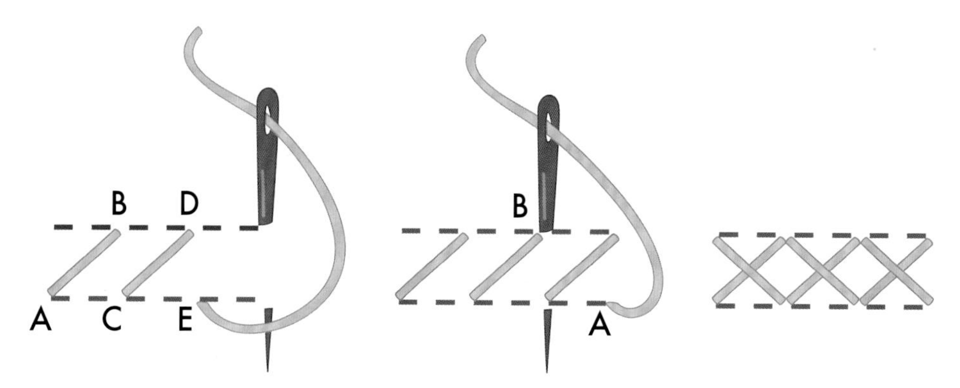

Satin stitch and long & short stitch

To make a **satin stitch**, pull the needle through to the right side of your fabric at **A**, then insert it at **B**. For a simple satin stitch, repeat this step with even stitches until you cover your space.

For a **long & short stitch** (which is often used to create lovely gradients), begin your first row by pulling your needle through at **A** then inserting at **B**. Continue the row, alternating long stitches (which will help you visualize the direction of your gradient) and short stitches side by side.

Repeat these steps for the second row.

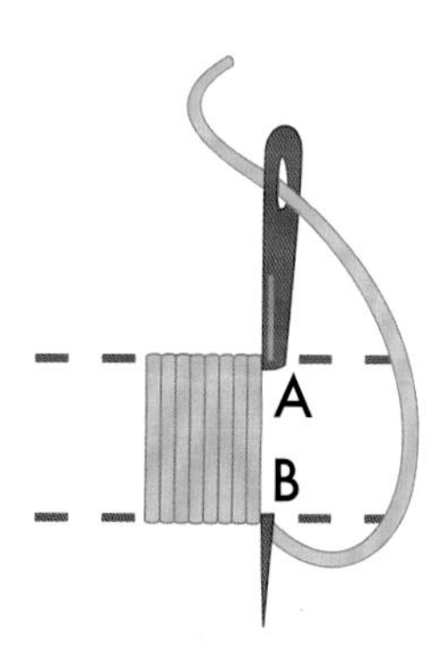

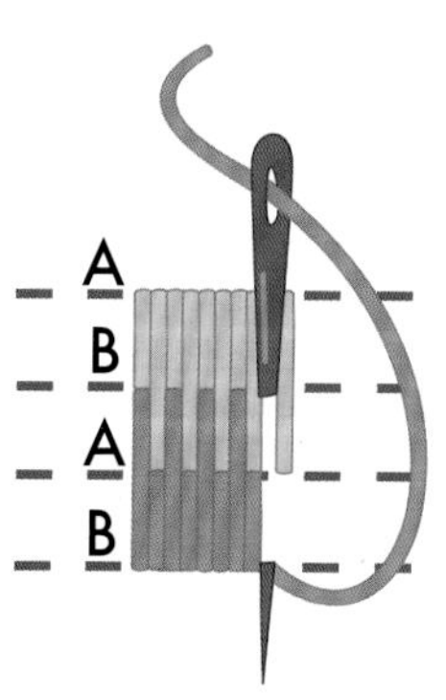

❸ Decorative stitches

These stitches are very nice to embroider and create pretty little designs.

Fly stitch

Pull the needle through to the right side of the fabric at **A**. Insert the needle at **B** and pull it out at **C**, so that the loop of your thread is held down by your needle.

Insert your needle at **D**, just below the loop so as to hold it in place.

Repeat these steps until you have covered your design.

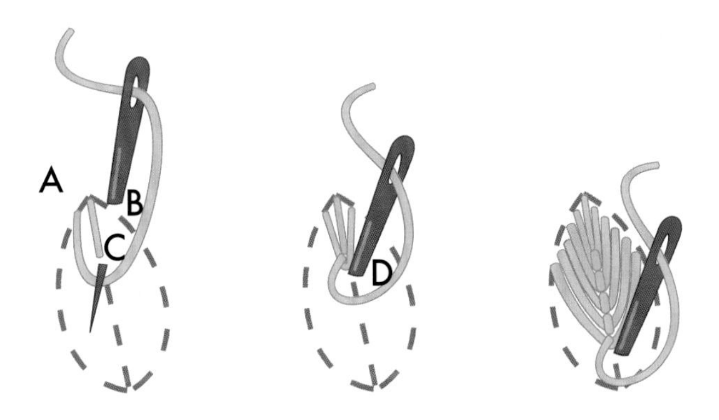

Star stitches: eyelet and Rhodes stitches

To make an **eyelet stitch**, pull your needle through to the right side of your fabric at **A**. Insert your needle at **B** and pull it out at **C**, reinsert at **B** and pull back out at **D**.

Continue these steps until you create an eyelet or **star** of however many rays you choose.

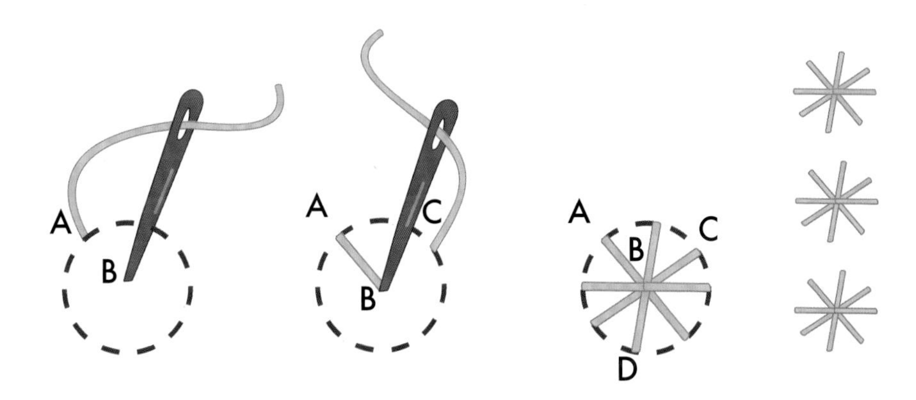

To make a circular Rhodes stitch, pull the needle through to the right side of the fabric at **A**. Insert your needle at **B** and pull it out at **C**, insert at **D** and pull it back out at **E**.

Repeat these steps until you complete your **circle**. The closer your stitches are, the more volume your star will have.

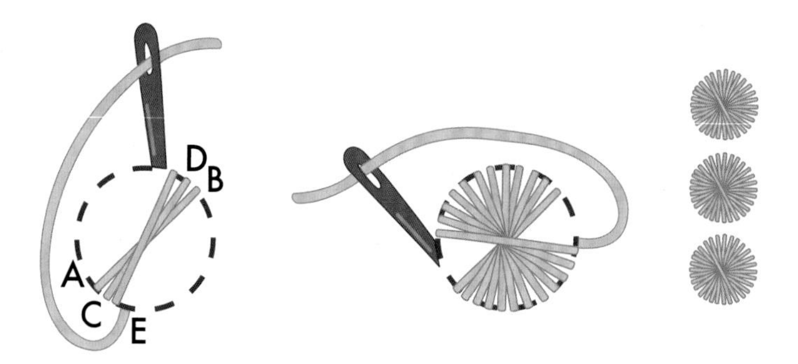

Feather stitch

To make a feather stitch, pull your needle through to the right side of your fabric at **A**, on the middle line. Form a loop to the right, inserting your needle at **B** and out again at **C**, so that the loop is held down by your needle.

Pull your needle downward and hold the stitch in place with your thumb. For a loop to the left, insert your needle at **D** and out again at **E**, repeating the same process until you have the desired length.

Finish your last loop with a tiny couching stitch.

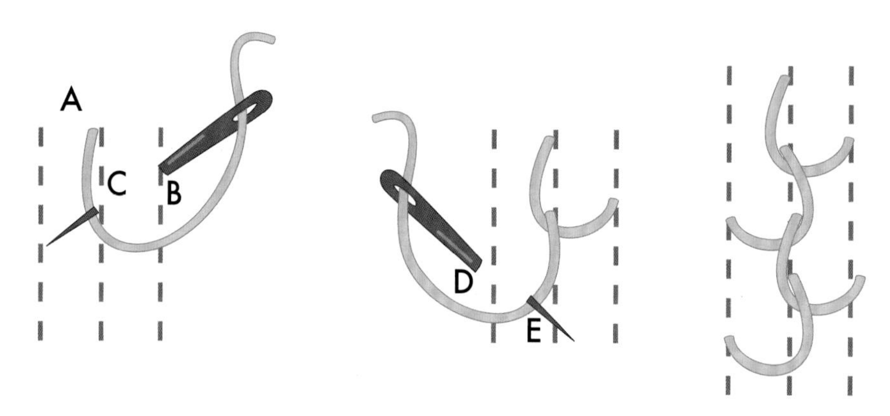

Fishbone stitch

To make a fishbone stitch, pull the needle through to the right side of the fabric at **A**. Insert the needle at **B**, slightly offset from the middle line, then pull the needle through at **C** and back down at **D**.

Repeat these steps, making sure that the inner ends of your stitches are always slightly offset from the center line, so that your stitches slightly overlap.

Repeat until you have covered your design.

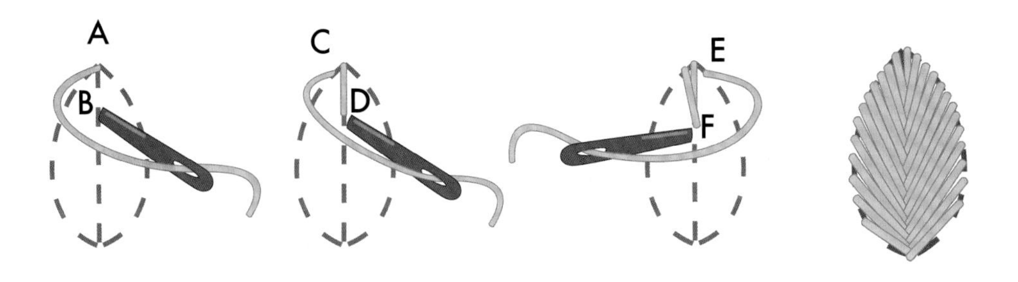

Lazy daisy

To make a lazy daisy, pull the needle through to the right side of the fabric at **A**. Insert the needle at **B** and pull it out at **C**, so that the loop of thread is held down by your needle.

Complete your little stitch by reinserting the needle at **D** to secure your loop in place.

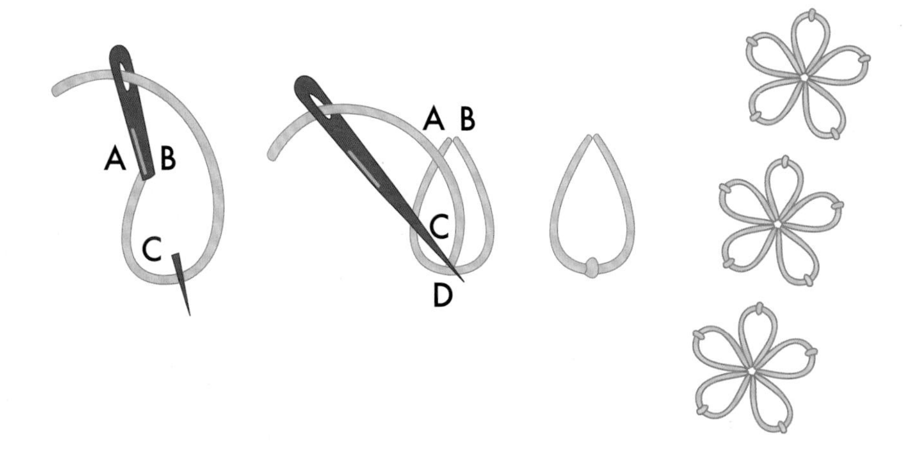

❸ Embellishments

These stitches let you add some volume and pizzazz to your embroidery.

French knots

To make a French knot, pull your needle through to the right side of the fabric at **A**.

Wrap your thread around your needle (2 or 3 times, depending on the size of knot you want), then insert your needle into the fabric again at **A**, holding onto the rest of your thread with your fingers in order to maintain the right tension.

Slide your thread through the **2 loops formed around the needle** under the **knot** forms on top of your fabric and the rest of your thread is below.

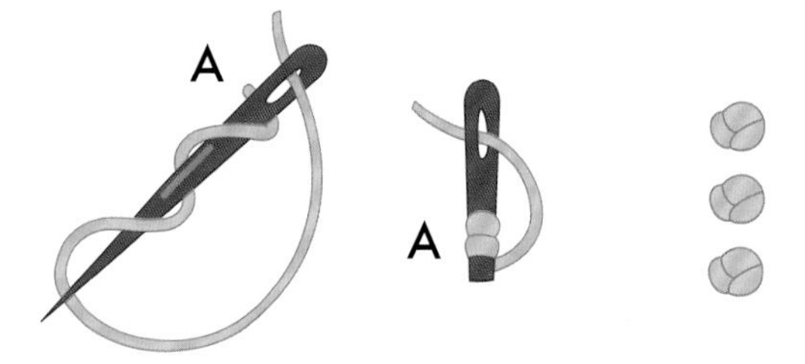

Bullion knots

To make a bullion knot, pull your needle through on the right side of your fabric at **A**. Then insert your needle behind it at **B**, and out again at **A**.

Leave your needle in the fabric (as shown in the diagram), and twist your thread around the pointed end of your needle, making tight loops. Make enough loops so that the length formed on your needle is the same as the distance from **A** to **B**.

Hold the loops between your fingers and gently slide your needle through, until all the loops are on the thread and your needle is free.

Insert the needle at **C** to finish the stitch.

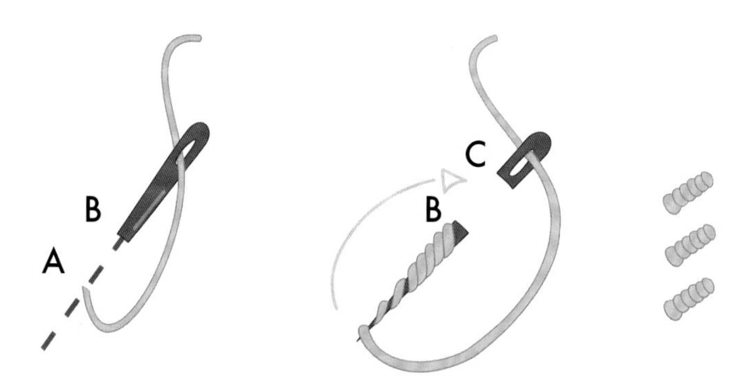

Woven wheel stitch

To make a woven wheel stitch, begin by stitching a **five-pointed eyelet star**, with each ray ending at the center of the circle.

Take another length of thread and pull it through to the right side of the fabric at **B**, making sure not to stitch through a ray of the star. You can use a rounded needle for this step.

Slide your needle over the first ray and under the second, never stitching into the fabric.

Continue weaving in this way until you can no longer see the rays of the star.

To complete the stitch, insert your needle under the last row and pull the thread through to the reverse side of your fabric.

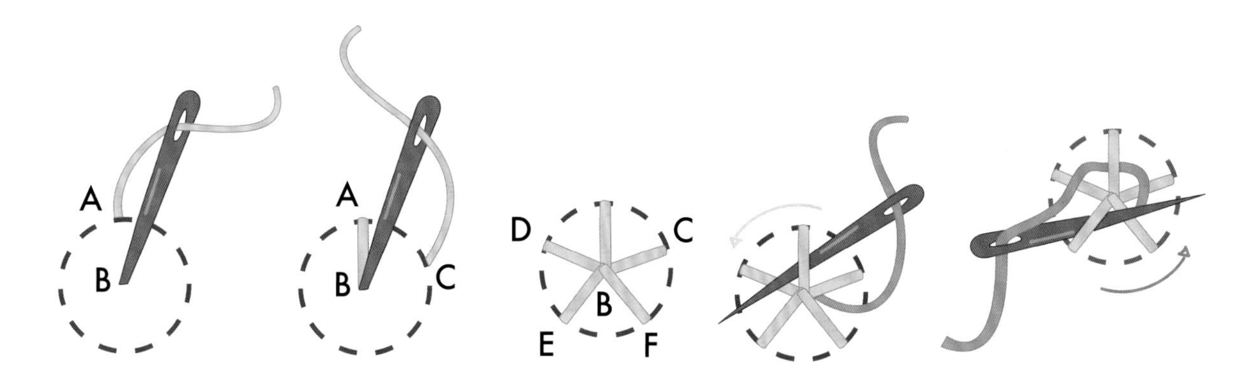

Tuft couching

To make a tuft or tassel, make a **little bundle of threads**. The number of strands depends on the result you want to achieve. Place them on your fabric and hold them in place with your finger.

Pull your needle through to the right side of your fabric at **A**. Make a small couching stitch by inserting your needle at **B**. Fold your little bundle in two and hold it in place with your finger. With your needle, **stitch from one side to the other** of your folded bundle from **C** to **D**. Make several more stitches like this one, from one side to the other of the little bundle.

For a nice finish, you can trim your bundled threads to an even length.

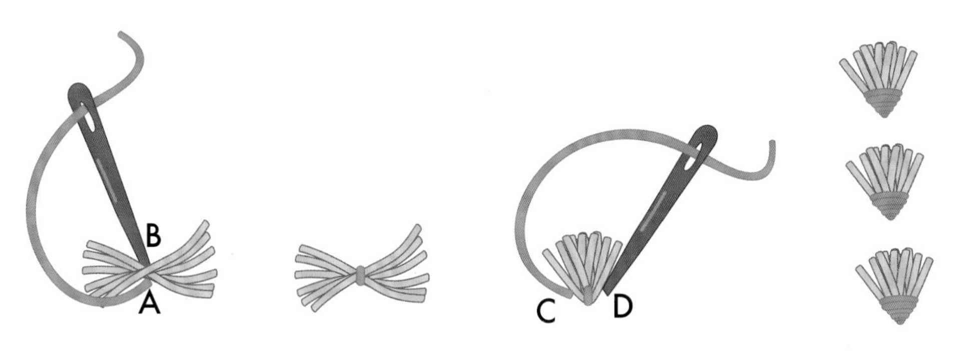

Beading

Now that you've learned all these pretty techniques for thread, it seems we now must talk about adding other decorative materials. Beads let your bring light, richness, and texture to your creations.

Beaded fringes

You can make two types of fringe.

❶ To make a fringe of beads, pull the needle through to the right side of the fabric at A.

String the number of beads you want for your fringe onto your thread.

Separate the last bead you strung, the one closest to your needle.

Now take your needle and slide it back through all the beads, except the one you've separated.

Reinsert your needle at A then secure your fringe by tying a knot on the reverse side of the fabric.

❷ Pull your needle through to the right side of your fabric at A. String your beads then insert your needle at B. Secure your fringe with a knot on the reverse side of the fabric.

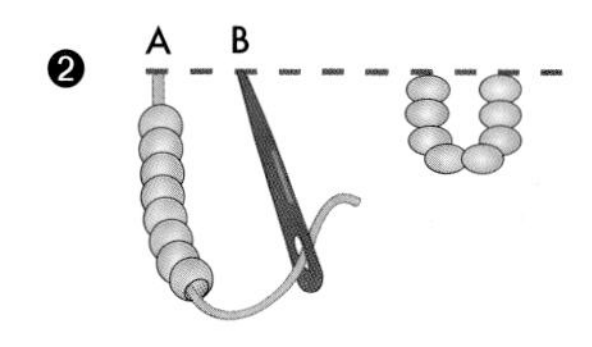

Scattered beads

To attach scattered beads, pull the needle through to the right side of the fabric at **A**, then string a bead.

Insert the needle at **B**.

Repeat for all of your scattered beads.

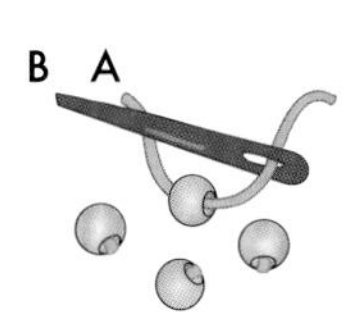

Back-stitched beads

❶ To attach beads using the back stitch, pull your needle through to the right side of the fabric at **A**, then string 2 beads and insert your needle at **B**.

❷ Pull your needle out at **C**, just in front of the last bead you have stitched.
Send your needle through this bead, then string 2 beads.
Insert your needle at **D**.

❸ Pull the needle out at **E**, just in front of the last bead you stitched and repeat the above steps.

❹ Continue until you have attached your line of beads.

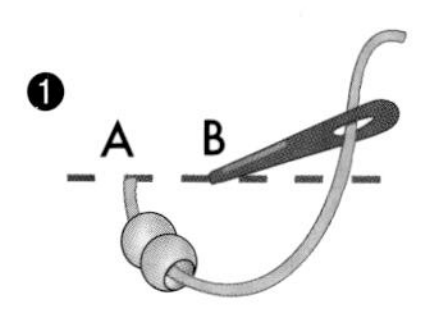

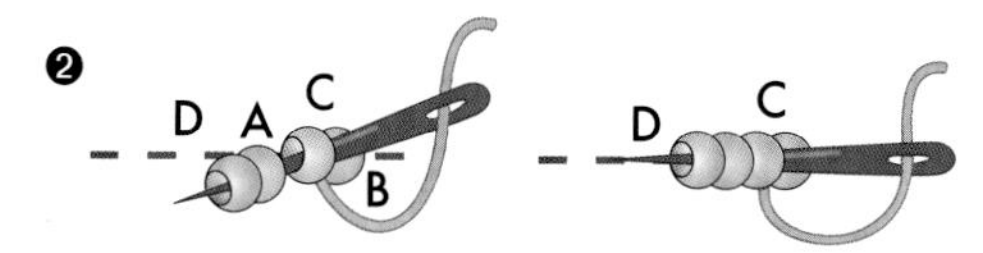

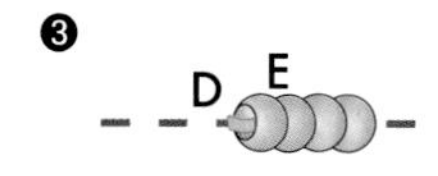

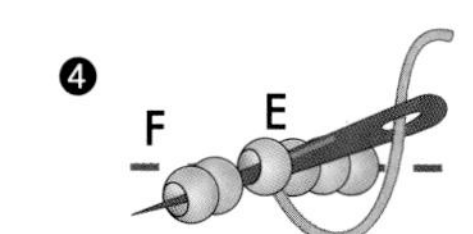

❸ Sequins

Now we'll look at a second kind of embellishment: sequins. They add a sparkling bejeweled quality to your most ambitious creations.

Double-stitched sequins

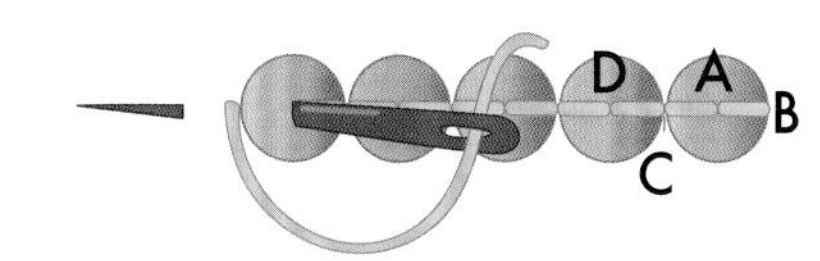

To attach a double-stitched sequin, pull your needle through to the right side of the fabric at **A**, then thread a sequin onto your needle. Insert your needle at B and pull it back out at **C**, then insert the needle again at **A**.

Repeat these steps until you have finished your line.

Beaded sequins

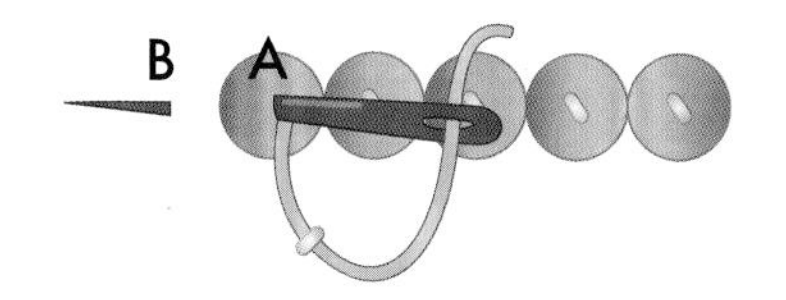

To attach sequins with a bead, pull the needle through to the right side of the fabric at **A**, string 1 sequin and 1 bead, and reinsert the needle back through the sequin at **A**.

Pull the needle back out at **B** and repeat the previous steps.

Continue until the end of the line.

Back-stitched sequins

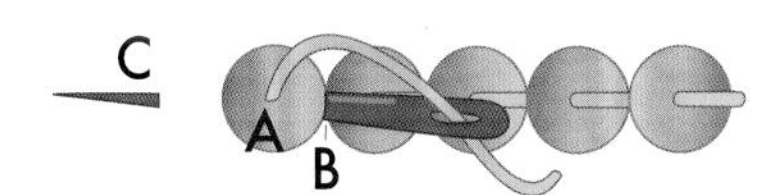

To attach sequins using a back stitch, pull the needle through to the right side of the fabric at **A**, then thread 1 sequin, insert the needle at **B**, and pull it back out at **C**. The distance from **A** to **C** should be the same as the sequin's diameter.

Continue these steps until the end of the line.

Overlapping sequins

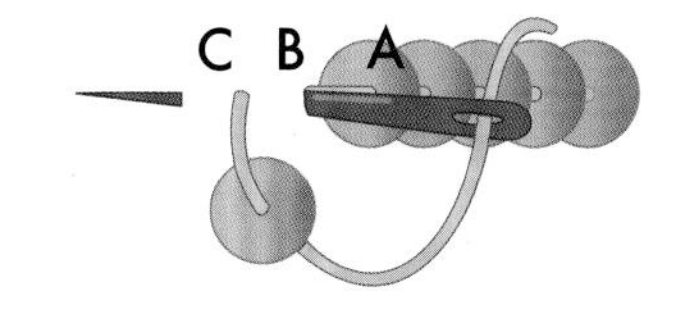

To attach overlapping sequins, begin by attaching your first sequin (this one will be attached in a different way from the rest). Pull your needle through to the right side of the fabric at **A**, string 1 sequin, then insert the needle at **B**.

The second sequin, as well as the rest in the line, will be attached in this way: pull your needle through at **C** so that the distance from **B** to **C** is equal to the sequin's radius. String a sequin and insert your needle at **B**. Attach the remaining sequins using a back stitch, making sure that the distance between your stitches causes your sequin to cover half the previous sequin.

Herbarium
Point avant
Point arrière
Point arrière fendu
Point de Boulogne
Point de chaînette
Point de feston
Point de tige
Point de croix
Passé plat
Point d'épine
Point d'étoile
Point de plume
Point de bouclettes
Point de poste
Point de velours
Franges de perles
Perles au point arrière
Sequins en deux points
Sequins à la perle

THE FRENCH HERBARIUM

CREATE A SAMPLER AS A LOVELY INTRODUCTION TO EMBROIDERY

A collection of stitches, in practice!

And now, let's embroider! This project is ideal for beginners, as it has small designs for different embroidery stitches to create a beautiful herbarium that will adorn your walls and serve both as study guide and stitch inventory for all your future work. It's like a little stroll through an enchanted forest of embroidery stitches.

You can also use any of these designs and techniques to decorate a nice tee-shirt, hat, pair of jeans...In short, anything your heart desires. The names of the stitches are provided in both French and English so that you can keep with the French theme in your descriptions if you wish.

Materials

- A large rectangle of natural cotton, about 25″ × 20″ (65 × 52cm)
- 2 wooden dowels 24″ (60cm)
- 30″ (75cm) of cotton string
- 4 wooden beads (here: 2 round green beads and 2 faceted beads in natural wood)
- DMC Six-Strand Embroidery Floss: the color numbers are listed for each design (following pages). Use the chart (at right) to take notes on any of your floss substitutions
- Seed beads: blue, light green, green, dark green, periwinkle, light pink, dark pink, light yellow
- Bugle beads: orange, pink
- Sequins: light yellow, yellow, violet, light pink, pink, dark pink, orange.

DMC number	Color description	Substitution floss
21	Alizarian, Light	
320	Pistachio Green, Medium	
347	Salmon, Very Dark	
367	Pistachio Green, Dark	
727	Topaz, Very Light	
761	Salmon, Light	
783	Topaz, Medium	
797	Royal Blue	
809	Delft Blue	
825	Blue, Dark	
893	Carnation, Light	
900	Burnt Orange, Dark	
913	Nile Green, Medium	
922	Copper, Light	
924	Gray Green, Very Dark	
988	Forest Green, Medium	
991	Aquamarine, Dark	
992	Aquamarine, Light	
3325	Baby Blue, Light	
3328	Salmon, Dark	
3340	Apricot, Medium	
3687	Mauve	
3705	Melon, Dark	
3809	Turquoise, Very Dark	
3816	Celadon Green	
3817	Celadon Green, Light	
3821	Straw	
3825	Pumpkin, Pale	
3836	Grape, Light	
3841	Baby Blue, Pale	
3847	Teal Green, Dark	
3849	Teal Green, Light	
3852	Straw, Very Dark	

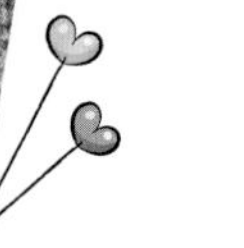

Instructions

Running stitch

This embroidery is done using the running stitch with a double thread.

- For the stem: DMC 320
- For the flowers:
  Petals: 809
  Pistils: 797
  Flower centers: 3821 Flower buds: 761
- For the leaves: 3816

Point avant

Running stitch

Whipped running stitch

This embroidery is done with a double thread.

- For the stems: whipped running stitch, 3809 and 3817
- For the flowers: whipped running stitch, 21 and 3836
- For the leaves: running stitch, 3809

Point avant mèche passée

Whipped running stitch

Back stitch

This embroidery is done with a double thread.

- For the yellow center: 3852
- For the orange petals: 3340
- For the dark pink: 893
- For the light pink: 761

Point arrière

Back stitch

Split back stitch

This embroidery is done with a double thread.

- For the stems: Alternate between colors 913 and 3816.
- For the center: 3809
- For the petals: Alternate between colors 347 and 3705.
- For the flower bud: 893

Point arrière fendu

Split back stitch

Couching stitch

This embroidery is done with a double thread.

- For the stems:
  Underlying thread: 924, couching stitches: alternate between colors 761 and 3836.
- For the clovers:
  Underlying thread: alternate between colors 367, 988, and 3847, couching stitches: alternate between colors 761 and 3836.

Point de Boulogne

Couching stitch

Chain stitch

This embroidery is done with a single strand.

- For the stem: 3816
- For the violet berries: 3836
- For the orange berries: 3825
- For the leaves: Alternate between colors 991 and 3816.

Point de chainette

Chain stitch

Blanket stitch

For this embroidery, the flowers are done with a double thread and the stems with a single strand.

- For the stems: chain stitch, alternate between colors 3816 and 3817.
- For the flowers: blanket stitch eyelets, alternate between colors 727 and 3821.

Point de feston

Blanket stitch

Stem stitch

This embroidery is done with a double thread.

- For the stems: 367
- For the leaves: Alternate between colors 988, 3816, 3817, and 3847.

Point de tige

Stem stitch

Cross stitch

This embroidery is done with a double thread.

- For the stem: 3816
- For the lightest leaf: 3817
- For the violet part of the flower: 3836
- For the pink part of the flower: 3687
- For the flower bud: 3687
- For the two-color leaf: 3816 and 3817

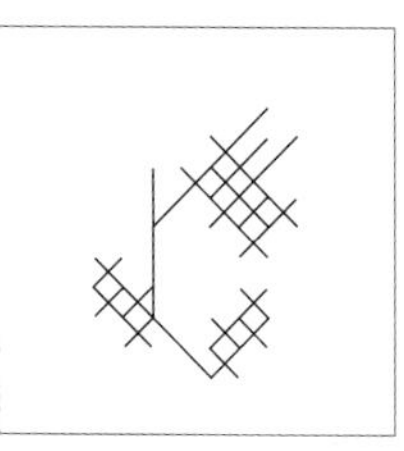

Point de croix

Cross stitch

Satin stitch and long & short stitch

For this embroidery, the flower is done with a double thread and the stem with a single strand.

- For the stem: chain stitch, 3817
- For the solid petals at the top: 900
- For the shaded petals on top: (from outside to inside) 922, then 761, then 783, then 900
- For the shaded petals on the bottom: (from outside to inside) 3825, then 761, then 783, then 900

Passé plat

Satin stitch

Fishbone stitch

For this embroidery, the leaves are done with a double thread and the stem with a single strand.

- For the stem: chain stitch, 3836
- For the leaves: fishbone stitch, alternate between colors 21, 922, and 3328.

Point d'arête

Fishbone stitch

Feather stitch

This embroidery is done with a double thread.

- Alternate between colors 809 and 3809.

Point d'épine

Feather stitch

Star stitches

For this embroidery, the flowers are done with a double thread and the stem with a single strand.

For the left flower

- For the stem: chain stitch, 988, and for the offshoots, alternate between colors 988 and 3817.
- For the flowers: eyelet stitch, alternate between colors 3836, 761, and 3821.

For the right flower

- For the stem: chain stitch, 3817, and for the offshoots, alternate between colors 3817 and 988.
- For the flowers: circular Rhodes stitch, alternate between colors 21, 761, and 3687.

Point d'étoile

Star stitches

Fly stitch

For this embroidery, the leaves are done with a double thread and the stem with a single strand.

- For the stems: chain stitch, alternate between colors 991 and 992.
- For the leaves: fly stitch, alternate between colors 991, 3816, and 3817.

Point de plume

Fly stitch

Lazy daisies

For this embroidery, the flowers are done with a double thread and the stems with a single strand.

- For the stems: chain stitch, alternate between colors 3816 and 3817.
- For the flowers: lazy daisy stitch, alternate between colors 727, 761, 3825, and 3836.
- For the leaves: lazy daisy stitch, alternate between colors 3816 and 3817.

Point de bouclette

Lazy daisies

French knots

For this embroidery, the flowers are done with a double thread and the stems with a single strand.

- For the stems: chain stitch, alternate between colors 3816 and 3817.
- For the violet circular flowers: French knots, 3836
- For the pink circular flowers: French knots, 761
- For the other flowers: French knots, 3687

Point de noeud

French knots

Bullion knots

For this embroidery, the flowers are done with a double thread and the stems with a single strand.

- For the stems: chain stitch, alternate between colors 3816 and 3841.
- For the light yellow flowers: bullion knots, 727, working outward from the center of the flower so that each petal runs along half of the previous stitch.
- For the darker yellow flowers: bullion knots, 783
- For the pink flowers: bullion knots, 761
- For the leaves: bullion knots, alternate between colors 3816 and 3841.

Point de poste

Bullion knots

Woven wheel stitch

For this embroidery, the flowers are done with a double thread.

- Alternate between colors: 761, 3340, 3687, and 3705

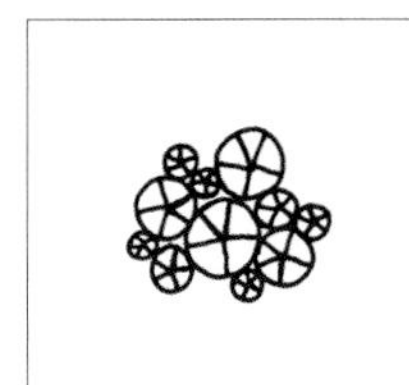

Point de roue

Woven wheel stitch

Tuft couching

For this embroidery, the base of the flowers is done with a double thread and the stems with a single strand.

- For the stems: chain stitch, alternate between colors 998, 3816, and 3817.
- For the flowers: tuft couching, alternate between colors 761, 783, 809, and 3852.

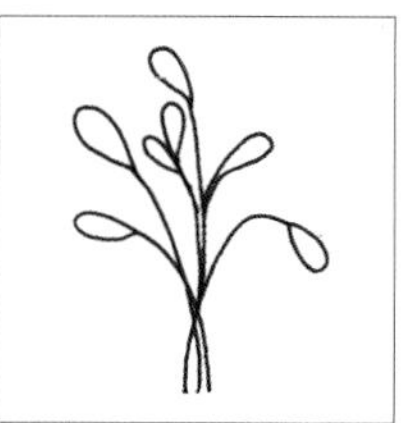

Point de velours

Tuft couching

Beaded fringes

For this embroidery, the fringes are attached with doubled sewing thread and the stems are embroidered with a single strand.

- For the embroidered vines: chain stitch, alternate between colors 988, 3816, 3817, and 3847.
- For the beaded fringes: alternate between blue, light green, and dark green seed beads.

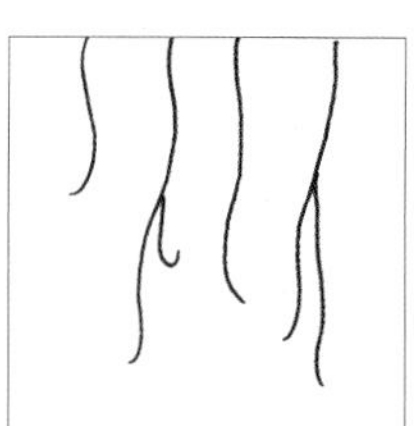

Franges de perles

Beaded fringes

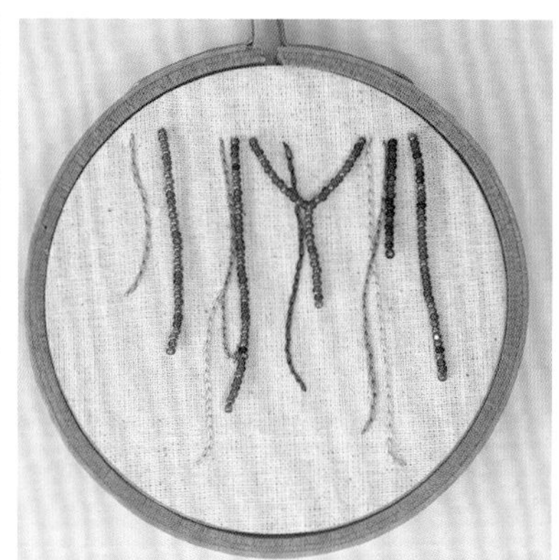

Scattered beads

For this embroidery, the beads are attached with a double thread and the stems are embroidered with a single strand.

- For the stems: chain stitch, alternate between colors 913 and 3817.
- For the flowers: scattered beads, periwinkle seed beads.

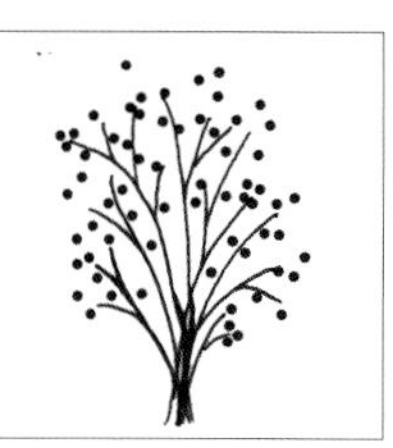

Perles à la puce

Scattered beads

Back-stitched beads

For this embroidery, the beads are attached with doubled sewing thread and the stems are embroidered with a single strand.

- For the stems: chain stitch, alternate between colors 809 and 3849.
- For the bell flowers: back stitch, orange bugle beads.
- For the pink flower: back stitch, pink bugle beads.
- For the leaves: back stitch, green seed beads.

Perles au point arrière

Back-stitched beads

Double-stitched sequins

For this embroidery, the sequins are attached with a double thread and the stem is embroidered with a single strand.

- For the stems: chain stitch, alternate between colors 3816 and 3817.
- For the sequins: double-stitched sequins, alternate between pink, yellow, and violet sequins and attach them with the thread matching their stems.

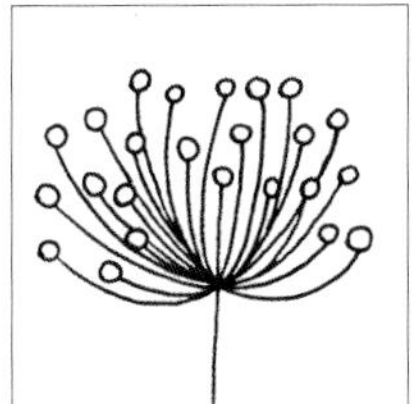

Sequins en deux points

Double-stitched sequins

Overlapping sequins

For this embroidery, the sequins are attached with doubled sewing thread and the stem is embroidered with a single strand.

- For the stem: chain stitch, 3817.
- For the flower: alternate between dark pink and light pink sequins every other petal.
- For the center: orange sequins.

Sequins au point rivière

Overlapping sequins

Beaded sequins

For this embroidery, the sequins are attached with doubled sewing thread and the stem is embroidered with a single strand.

- For the stems: chain stitch, alternate between colors 367, 992, and 3817.
- For the blue flowers: blue sequins each topped with a blue seed bead.
- For the dark pink flower: dark pink sequins each topped with a dark pink seed bead.
- For the light pink flower: light pink sequins each topped with a light pink seed bead.
- For the light yellow flower: light yellow sequins each topped with a light yellow seed bead.

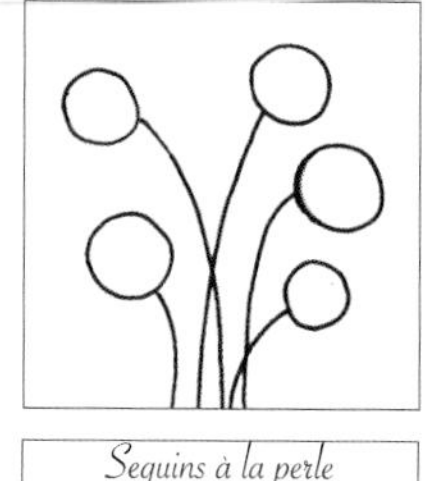

Sequins à la perle

Beaded sequins

Embroidering the letters

Embroider the title using a chain stitch, with a single strand of 825. To create the different thicknesses, embroider several lines of chain stitch until your embroidery matches the example shown.

Assembly

1 Fold the two shorter sides ¼″ (0.5cm) from the edge and crease with an iron.

2 Fold the two longer sides ¼″ (0.5cm) from the edge, crease with an iron, then fold again. Sew the length of the sides by hand or machine.

3 Return to the shorter sides and fold them 1″ (2cm) from the edge (as you need this tube large enough to hold your wooden dowels, this measurement may need to be adjusted). Sew these two sides as close as possible to the edge of the hem.

4 Slide your wooden dowels through these fabric tubes.

5 Last, take your string, thread the wooden beads at each end, and attach the string to the upper dowel.

QUICK GUIDE for nicely finishing YOUR PROJECTS

REMOVE THE SOLUBLE PAPER OR FRICTION PEN, CLOSE THE BACK OF YOUR HOOP, DECORATE THE HOOP...

You did it! You've finished your first embroidery, congratulations!
Now let's take care of some little finishing touches to make the final result impeccable.

Tidying up the back

First off, before you take your work out of the embroidery hoop or frame, you can turn it over and tidy up the back. This means cutting all the little thread tails to ¼" (0.5cm) from the knots holding them in place.

If you've inadvertently created little loops on the reverse side of your embroidery, fret not—we can take care of them. Take a double thread and knot the end. Slide it through one of your passes and wrap it around this thread. Now grab your little accidental loop and, with your thread, pin it against the back of the fabric and knot in place.

Remove pen and marker marks

If you've chosen to work with heat-erasable pens or markers, before taking your work out of your embroidery hoop or frame, use the steam from your iron to make your drawn-on design disappear. If some little marks remain, you can use the tip of the iron and delicately remove those tiny troublemakers.

Remove the water-soluble stabilizer or magic paper

If you have chosen to work with water-soluble stabilizer or magic paper, now is the time to remove it. Submerge your work in water and swish it around a little, then wring out your fabric. So as not to damage your embroidery, the best method is to roll your piece in a towel, then step on it to get out as much water as possible. Lay the embroidery flat to dry. If, once dry, your fabric still seems a little stiff, repeat this process.

Pressing your work

You can press your embroidery using one of **three methods**.

- The first method involves using a damp cloth. Take a piece of white cotton fabric, perhaps a square from an old sheet, soak it with water, and wring it out so it no longer drips. Place this cloth between your iron and the back of your embroidery. You can now iron your damp cloth, then remove it. Wait until your work is cool and dry before moving it. The damp cloth gives some volume to your thread and helps you avoid smoothing or flattening your stitches.

TIP

Once the embroidery hoop is removed, if the fabric around your embroidery is puckering from thread tension—which can happen with stitches like the chain stitch or long & short stitch—stretch your fabric back out and use a damp cloth. If you do this correctly, you should be able to relax those little wrinkles around your embroidery.

- The second method involves placing **a sheet of parchment paper** between your iron and your embroidery and ironing on the reverse side.
- You can also **iron** your embroidery **by using the steam setting on the reverse side**. Make sure that the sole plate of your iron is perfectly clean and not coated with limescale!

❻ *Hoop Art finishes*

Hoop Art involves keeping your embroidery hoop as the frame for your finished embroidery. You can find all kinds of embroidery hoops to bring your ideas to life.

For Hoop Art, you have **two finishing methods**.

- For the first, the back of your embroidery will be visible, so don't skip the step of tidying up the reverse side. Take your embroidery and place the outer circle on the reverse side. Using a ruler, make marks about 1" to 2" (2 to 4cm) from the outer circle of your hoop. Cut the fabric following these marks. You can now reassemble your embroidery hoop with your fabric. Prepare a very long double thread (2 times the circumference of your hoop), then make long running stitches ½" (1cm) from the edge of your fabric. Evenly distribute the little folds that are formed, then make a strong knot.

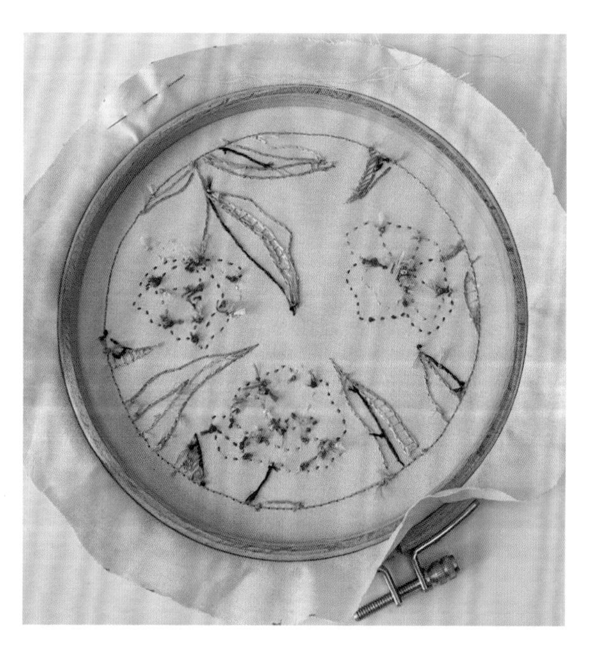

For the second method, you will hide **the back of your embroidery**, so you do not have to do any serious tidying up, even if it never hurts. Begin by removing your embroidery hoop, then take the inner circle and trace its outline on a piece of felt in whichever color you choose, then cut it. Now complete the previous method. Once you have sewn the back of your fabric, take the piece of felt, position it on the reverse of your embroidery along the inner circle of your hoop, then pin it in place. Use the blanket stitch to sew the felt to your fabric, with even stitches and with the spikes of the blanket stitch pointing toward the center of the circle.

TIP

Hoop Art also gives you the opportunity to let your creativity run wild when it comes to decorating your embroidery hoop. You can paint it: once your embroidery is finished (and absolutely not before), remove your embroidery hoop, paint it in the color or colors of your choosing and let it dry completely before putting your embroidery back inside. You can add macramé, pompoms, ribbons, thread, or yarn. You can even attach dried flowers, plastic beads, wooden beads, shells... Have fun!

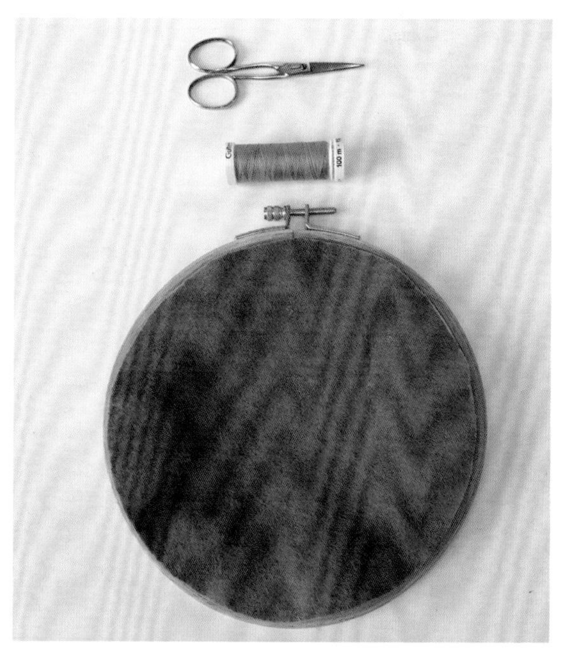

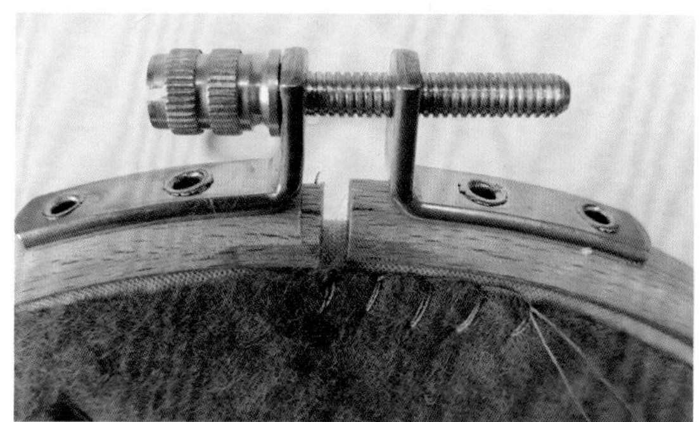

WHOLEHEARTEDLY

WORK ON YOUR PRECISION

Complete an embroidered design and its mirror image on a blouse or shirt.

Today, I'm giving you a challenge! You need to embroider the exact same design twice on two sides of a piece of clothing... In order to succeed, from positioning your design through its stitching, you will need to compare the two sides constantly. Precision and concentration are of the essence! Don't shy from being meticulous, work with regularity, and count all the stitches that make up your flowers to achieve a perfect mirror effect.

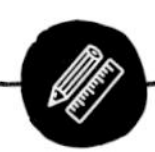

Materials

A light blue shirt • DMC Six-Strand Embroidery Floss 782 and 825

Stitches

Stem stitch • Back stitch • Fishbone stitch • Satin stitch

DMC number	Color description	Substitution floss
782	Topaz, Dark	
825	Blue, Dark	

Instructions

1 Begin by transferring your designs onto each side of your piece of clothing. If you have chosen a button-up shirt, place them on the chest, aligning the hearts with a buttonhole. If like me you've chosen a blouse, position the hearts on each side of the chest, making sure they are the same distance from the side seams. You can position the little branch at the shoulder or at the base of the sleeves.

2 Position your embroidery hoop around the heart design so that the design is not warped and the fabric is nice and tight.

3 Embroider the **heart** and **flames** using the stem stitch with a double thread of 825.

4 Then embroider the rays using a back stitch with a double thread of 825 (these stitches will cross over the flames).

5 Now embroider the **flower stems**, except the central stem, using a back stitch with a double thread of 825.

6 Embroider the **central stem** using the stem stitch with a double thread of 825.

7 All the **leaves** are embroidered using a slightly altered fishbone stitch. Instead of overlapping the stitches in the middle, have all your stitches terminate at the same point at the base of each leaf.

8 Embroider all the **flowers** using a vertical satin stitch with a double thread of 782.

9 You can now move your embroidery hoop to the sleeve and embroider the **branch** using a back stitch with a double thread of 825.

Finally, create the mirror image of what you have just embroidered, following all the advice I've given you; it's all a matter of concentration... It's your turn now!

Enlarge 147%

MASTER ONE OF THE GREAT EMBROIDERY CLASSICS

Cross stitch.

To wrap up this first week of embroidery, I present to you an embroidery project using cross stitch. This stitch, which was already being used as far back at the 9th century and truly blossomed in the Middle Ages, is an embroidery essential. During the Renaissance, this artform spread across Europe, and it continued to evolve through the 1980s with innovations in dyeing, traditions for educating young women, new ways of using old patterns, the success of pattern grids and printed fabrics, up to the version we now know today. By picking up your needle today, you are inscribing yourself in this long history.

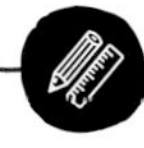

Materials

18 count Aida cloth (7 pts/cm) • DMC Six-Strand Embroidery Floss 340, 597, 725, 727, 744, 745, 747, 793, 800, 825, 893, 922, 992, 3328, 3340, 3705, 3713, 727, 3816, 3817, 3825 • 6" (15.5cm) embroidery hoop

Stitches

Cross stitch

340	745	893	3705	3825
597	747	922	3713	
725	793	992	3727	
727	800	3328	3816	
744	825	3340	3817	

DMC number	Color description	Substitution floss
340	Blue Violet, Medium	
597	Turquoise	
725	Topaz	
727	Topaz, Very Light	
744	Yellow, Pale	
745	Yellow, Light Pale	
747	Sky Blue, Very Light	
793	Cornflower Blue, Medium	
800	Delft Blue, Pale	
825	Blue, Dark	
893	Carnation, Light	
922	Copper, Light	
992	Aquamarine, Light	
3328	Salmon, Dark	
3340	Apricot, Medium	
3705	Melon, Dark	
3713	Salmon, Very Light	
3727	Antique Mauve, Light	
3816	Celadon Green	
3817	Celadon Green, Light	
3825	Pumpkin, Pale	

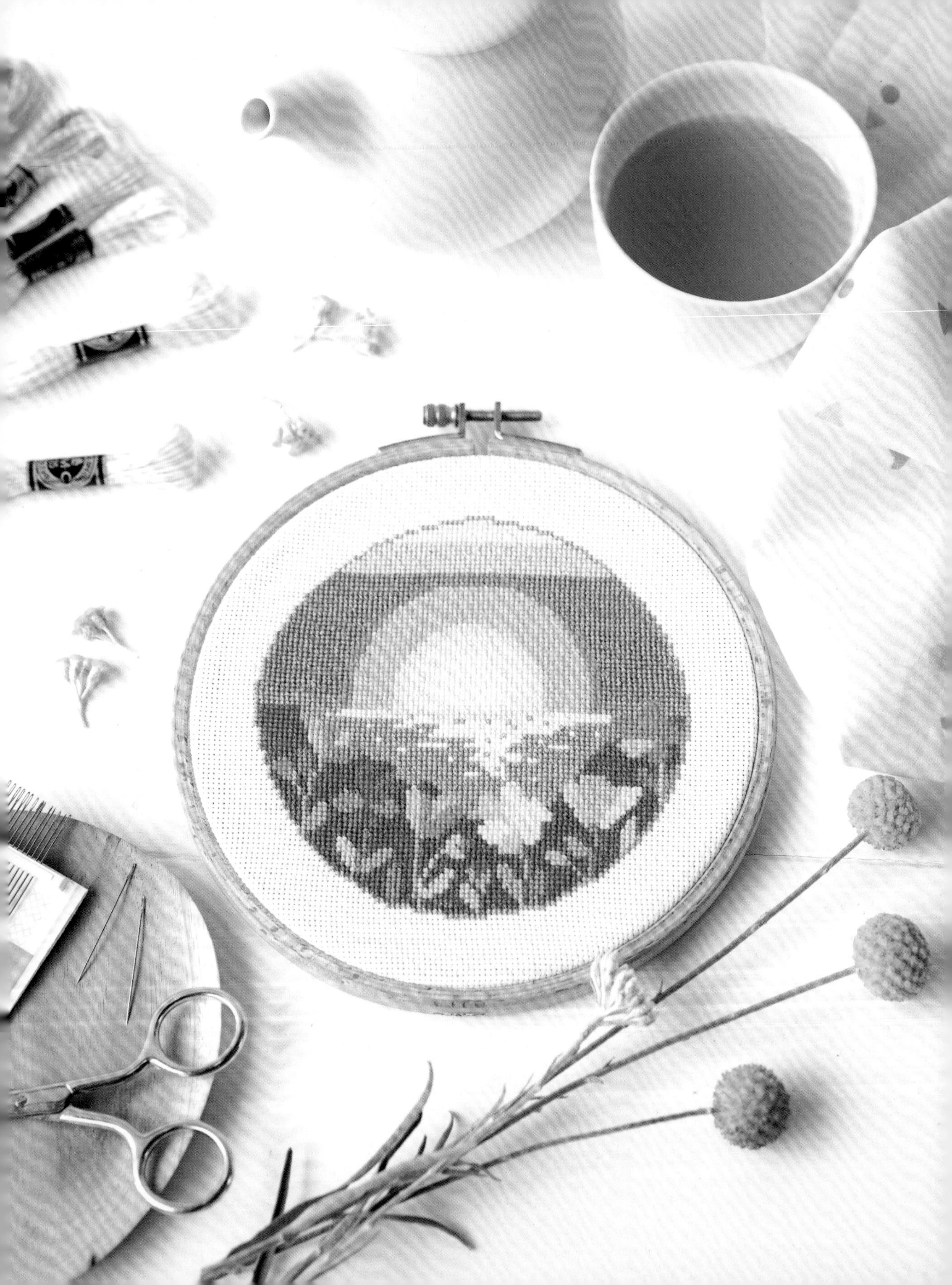

× LITTLE REMINDERS FOR THIS LESSON

- To achieve a nice effect, choose one direction for your cross stitching and maintain it throughout your embroidery: if your second stitch, the one that completes the cross, is oriented from the top left to the bottom right, keep this orientation until the end.
- Don't forget to read the last part of the lesson on Day 5 for how to perfectly finish your embroidery.

Instructions

Follow the design according to the grid (enlarge 182%).

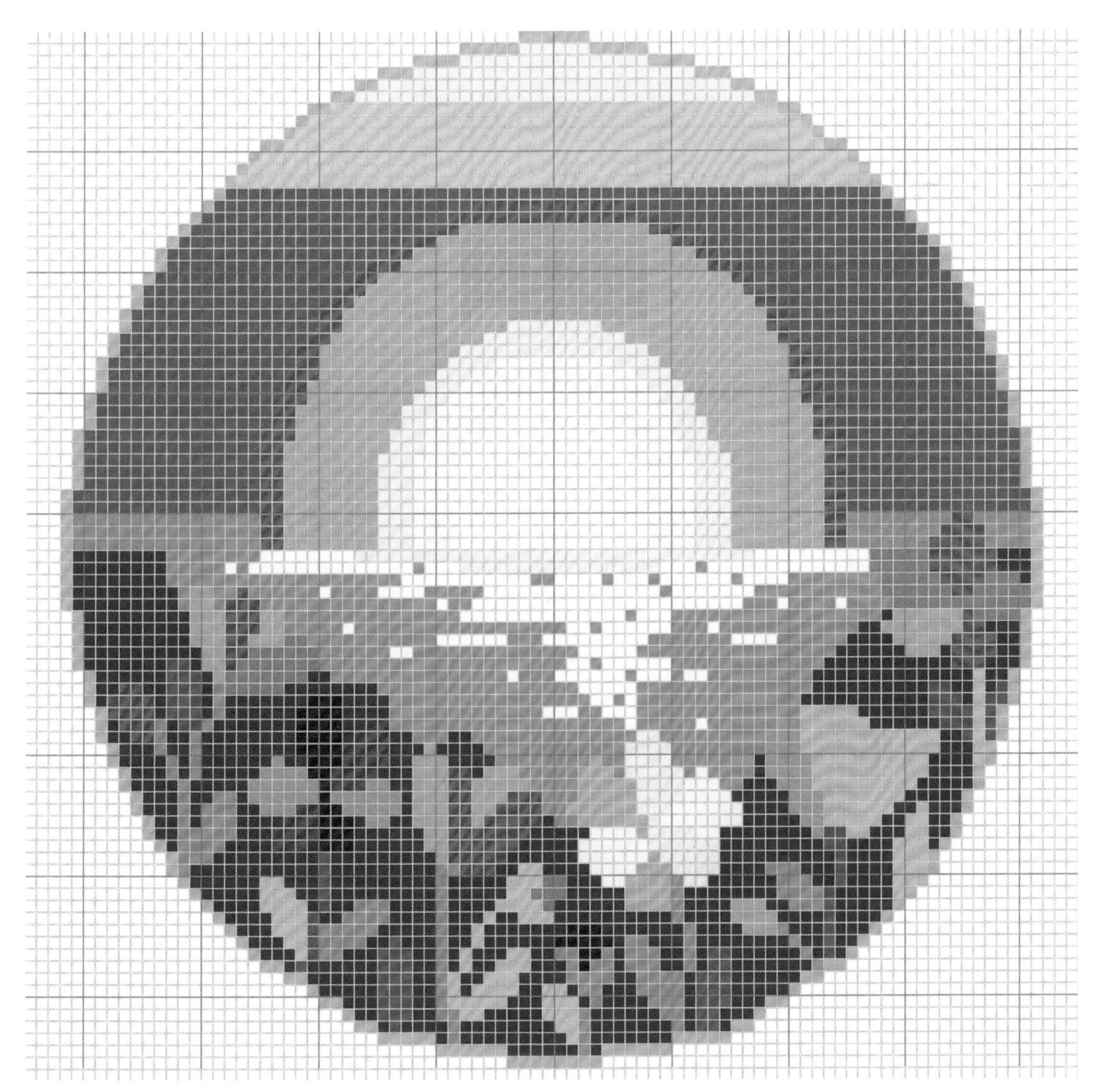

MASTER EMBROIDERY ON STRETCH FABRIC

Ah, embroidering stretchy fabric, what a wonderful lesson for this first day of our second week! It's totally normal to want to embroider your own tee-shirts as soon as you understand the basics. So to satisfy this desire, we're going to start this lesson with some brief technical pointers about embroidering on stretch fabric. The issue with this fabric is that it puckers easily. To avoid this, you have to pay close attention at every step.

Start by washing and drying your fabric or article of clothing, as jersey often shrinks in the wash.

❶ *Choose your method...*

To help you tame the fabric's stretchiness, there are three highly practical methods: interfacing, water-soluble stabilizer, and adhesive water-soluble stabilizer.

The first method uses **fusible interfacing**, which adds stability to your fabric.

Position the bumpy side of the interfacing against the reverse side of your jersey, then iron, without steam, for several minutes, pressing evenly. Wait until the glue is completely set. This fabric will remain on your clothing.

This is not my favorite method, as the interfacing doesn't hold up well after repeated washing and it adds thickness to your fabric.

The second method uses **water-soluble stabilizer**. You can use this in two ways:

- The first is to trace your design on the water-soluble stabilizer then attach it to your fabric using a basting stitch* before putting it into the embroidery hoop. Basting allows you to control the tension of the jersey in the embroidery hoop, and the water-soluble stabilizer lets your embroider more comfortably as it lends stability to your fabric.
- The second involves stretching the water-soluble stabilizer in your embroidery hoop like fabric, then pinning your stretch fabric onto it, onto which you will transfer your design. The pins hold your fabric in place without pulling on the fabric, and the water-soluble stabilizer lends stability to your fabric.

As the name suggests, you can then remove the water-soluble stabilizer in water.

The third method, the most beginner-friendly of the three, uses **adhesive water-soluble stabilizer**. It's a very effective way to stabilize your stretch fabrics.

Transfer your design to the paper, then stick it to your fabric on a flat surface, before putting the fabric in the embroidery hoop. The paper's adhesive holds the fabric's weave in place, preventing it from warping. The paper is relatively rigid, thus allowing you to embroider at ease. This paper can be easily removed with water, just like water-soluble stabilizer.

* Basting stitch: hand-stitching similar to long, relaxed running stitches to temporarily assemble pieces that will later be permanently sewn together.

TIP

- When you assemble your embroidery hoop or frame, you should make absolutely sure that your fabric is flat, that the grainline is straight, and above all that you are not stretching your fabric: it must remain relaxed.
- Make sure to always remove your embroidery hoop between embroidery sessions so that it dœsn't leave marks on your fabric.

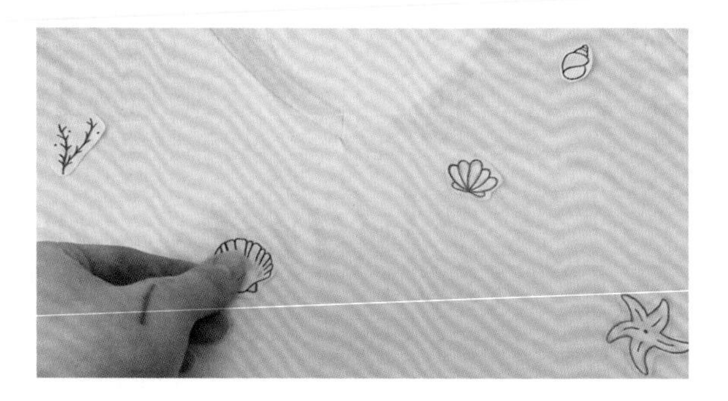

Materials

A pink tee-shirt • DMC Six-Strand Embroidery floss: 444, 445, 608, 747, 893, 964, 992, 993, 3340, 3809

Stitches

Split back stitch • French knots • Feather stitch

DMC number	Color description	Substitution floss
444	Lemon, Dark	
445	Lemon, Light	
608	Orange, Bright	
747	Sky Blue, Very Light	
893	Carnation, Light	
964	Seagreen, Light	
992	Aquamarine, Light	
993	Aquamarine, Very Light	
3340	Apricot, Medium	
3809	Turquoise, Very Dark	

Instructions

1 Since my fabric is particularly soft and stretchy, I decided to combine two methods which you have already seen. You can do the same if you're in a similar situation; otherwise, I recommend simply using the **adhesive stitch stabilizer method** as described above.

Transfer your designs (page 59) onto a sheet of stitch stabilizer.

2 **Cut them out individually and stick them** onto your fabric, positioning them in a way that looks natural to you. If your fabric is like mine, take a large embroidery hoop covered with water-soluble stabilizer and pin each design to the stretched stabilizer. Otherwise, use a small hoop and position it around your first design, then move reposition it for each following design.

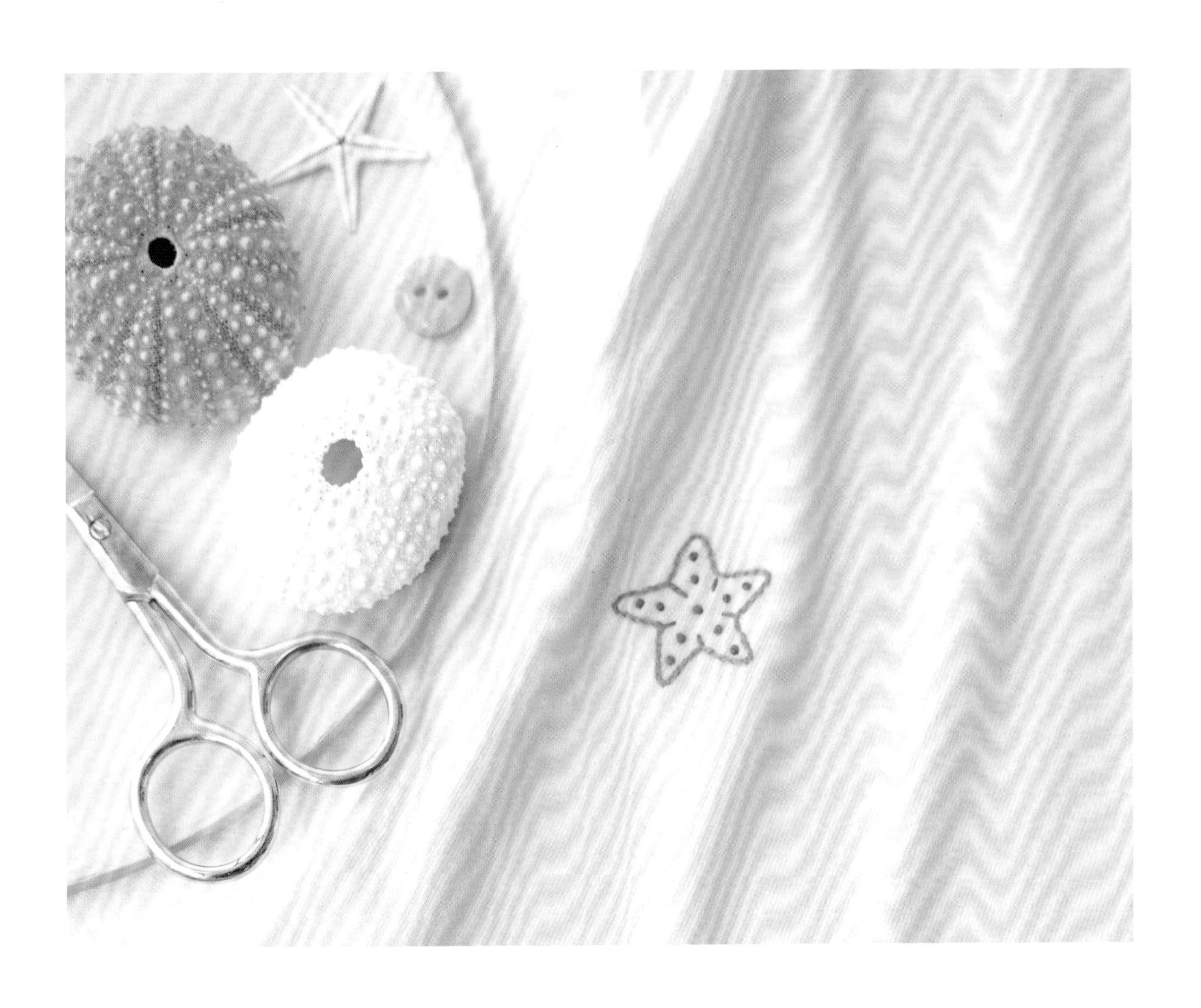

Enlarge 156%

3 Begin by **embroidering** the **3 bubbles in 1** using the split back stitch with a double thread. The **upper bubble** is embroidered in 444, the **left bubble** in 445, and the **right bubble** in 747.

4 Next embroider:

- **shell 2** using the split back stitch with a double thread, the **main shell** in 3727 and the **little fins** on the side in 893,
- **shell 3** using the split back stitch with a double thread, alternating between 3340 and 608,
- **shell 4** using the split back stitch with a double thread, alternating between 893 and 3809, **starting at the bottom** of the shell with the lighter thread.

5 Next embroider **seaweed 5** using the feather stitch with a double thread, the **left branch** in 3814 and the **right branch** in 992.

6 Continue with the outline of **star 6** using the split back stitch with a double thread of 3340, then create the spots using French knots with a double thread of 608 (2 twists around the needle).

7 Now embroider **shell 7** using the split back stitch with a double thread, alternating between 444 and 445, **starting at the bottom** of the shell with the darker thread.

8 Continue with the outline of **star 8** using the split back stitch with a double thread of 3727, then embroider the **grooves** using a running stitch with a double thread of 893. Last, create a **French knot** using a double thread of 3727 (2 twists around the needle).

9 Embroider the outline of **star 9** using the split back stitch with a double thread of 3809, then the **grooves** using the split back stitch with a double thread of 964, and lastly, make a **French knot** using a double thread of 3809 (2 twists around the needle).

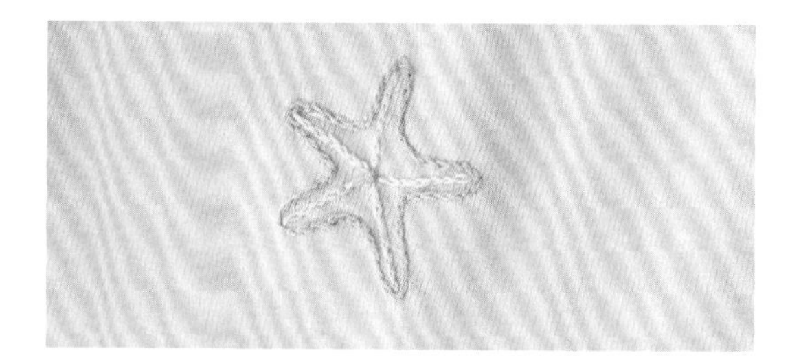

10 Embroider **shell 10** using the split back stitch with a double thread of 3340, then the grooves using the split back stitch with a double thread of 608.

11 Embroider the **4 bubbles** in 11 using the split back stitch with a double thread of 893, 964, and 3809 in whichever order you prefer.

12 To finish, **submerge your piece of clothing in water** and let it swish around for a few seconds until you're sure all the glue is gone. **Lay your clothing flat** on a towel. If you see that there is some tension between the fabric and thread, gently pull on your stitches until the fabric relaxes. Next, roll up the towel with your flat clothing inside. Once it's all rolled up, you can step on it to **extract the water** without damaging your work. Unroll the towel and **lay your clothing flat to dry.**

You now know how to embroider on stretch fabrics and can personalize your tee-shirts to your heart's content.

BETWEEN THE LINES

DRAW INSPIRATION FROM A JAPANESE CLASSIC TO EMBROIDER A PILLOW

To continue your lessons, I offer you a Sashiko-inspired project, as this technique is one that uses a very simple base stitch—the running stitch—and it's a classic of traditional Japanese embroidery.

What we will do here is not exactly Sashiko, because we won't be following all the rules, but it is still a project that draws inspiration from that technique.

And now, make a wish and away we go!

Brief historical note

The Sashiko technique is an embroidery technique using the running stitch that most likely began in Japan during the first century C.E., and then further developed around the 1600s. It is used for reinforcing and repairing clothing, and is sometimes considered a lucky charm for whoever wears it. Over time, Sashiko and its refined lines have become a decorative practice.

Materials

2 squares 16" × 16" (40 × 40cm) of opaque aqua fabric • Pillow stuffing • DMC Six-Strand Embroidery Floss: 225, 747, 959, 964, 3340, 3706, 3842

Stitches

Running stitch • French knots

DMC number	Color description	Substitution floss
225	Shell Pink, Ultra Very Light	
747	Sky Blue, Very Light	
959	Seagreen, Medium	
964	Seagreen, Light	
3340	Apricot, Medium	
3706	Melon, Medium	
3842	Wedgewood, Dark	

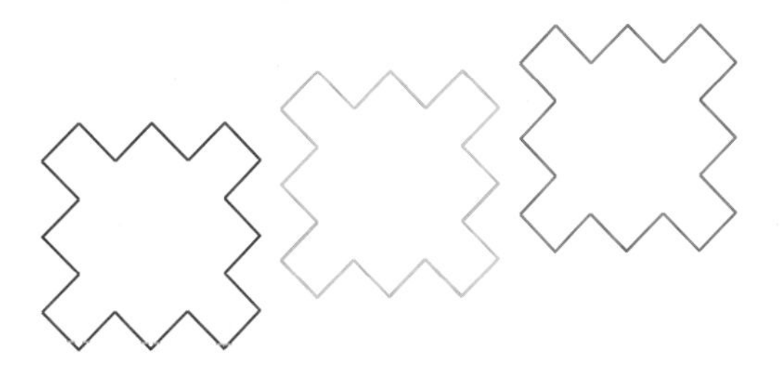

Instructions

1 To embroider this pillow, you will need to work a line of color at a time, following the design opposite. Trace the complete design onto your fabric.

2 Position your embroidery hoop or assemble your frame.

3 Embroider the designs, referring to the diagrams below. The **orange** part of the enlarged design corresponds to **diagram ❶** (below). The **yellow** part corresponds to **diagram ❷**. The **pink** part corresponds to **diagram ❸**. All the **geometric forms** are embroidered using the **running stitch with a double thread** and the little **circles** are embroidered using **French knots with a triple thread** (2 twists around the needle).

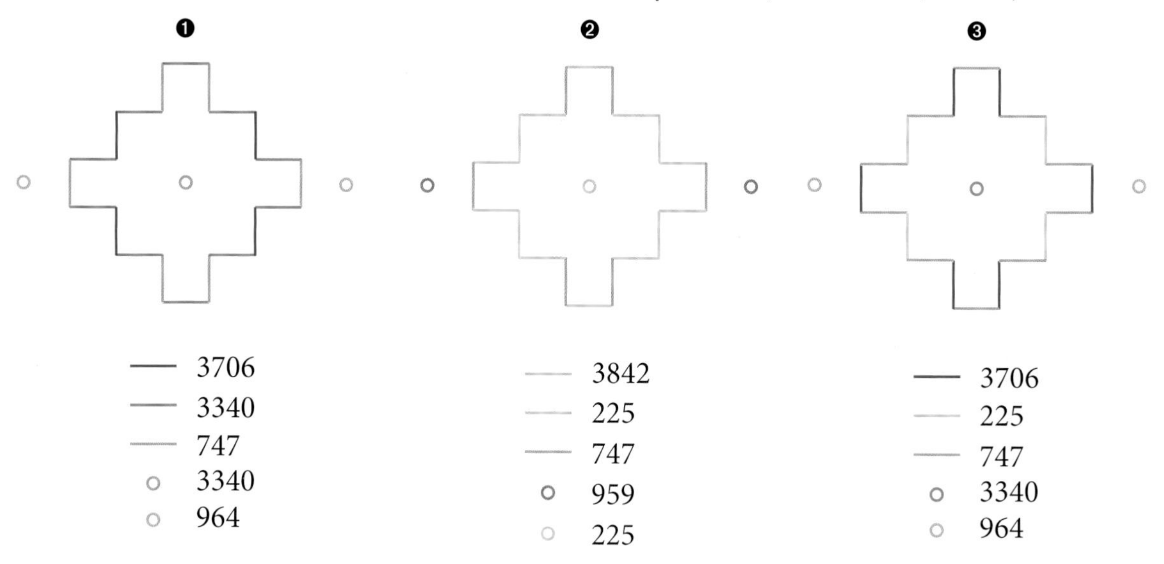

Assembly

1 Cut your fabric ½″ (1cm) from the edge of your embroidery, then cut the same shape in your second fabric square.

2 Position your fabrics with right sides together, then sew all around your square, ½″ (1cm) from the edge, leaving a 4″ (10cm) opening.

Trim your corners.

3 Turn your work right side out and give it a quick iron. Fill your pillow case with stuffing and close the opening with a small invisible stitch.

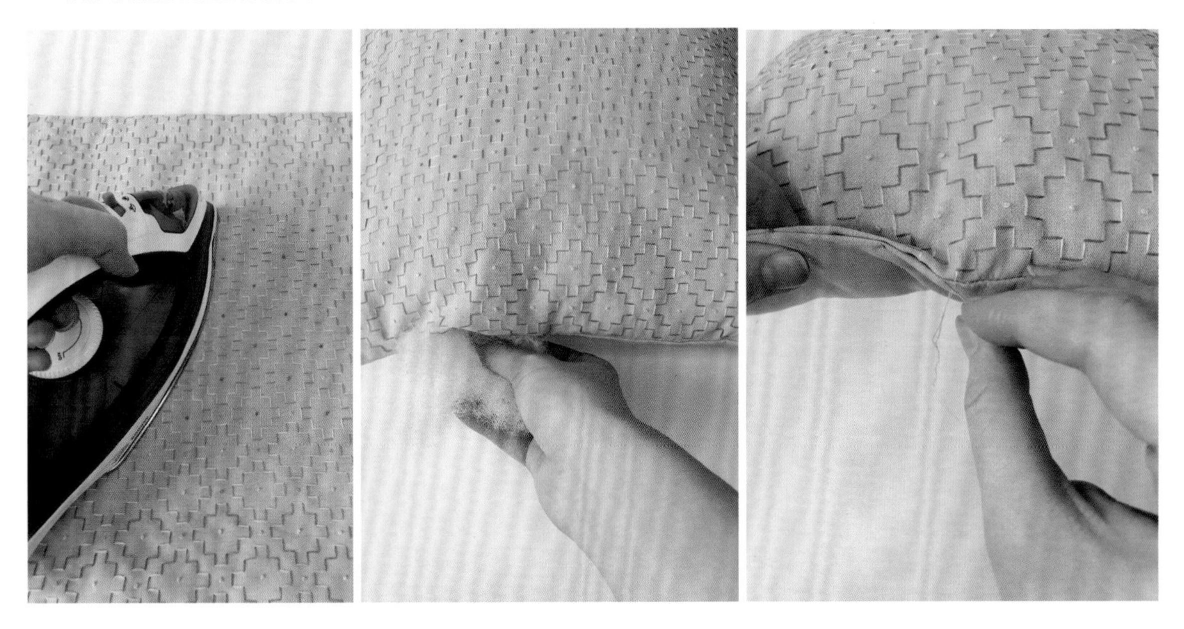

Sashiko is a very pretty technique for decorating your home.

Enlarge 454%

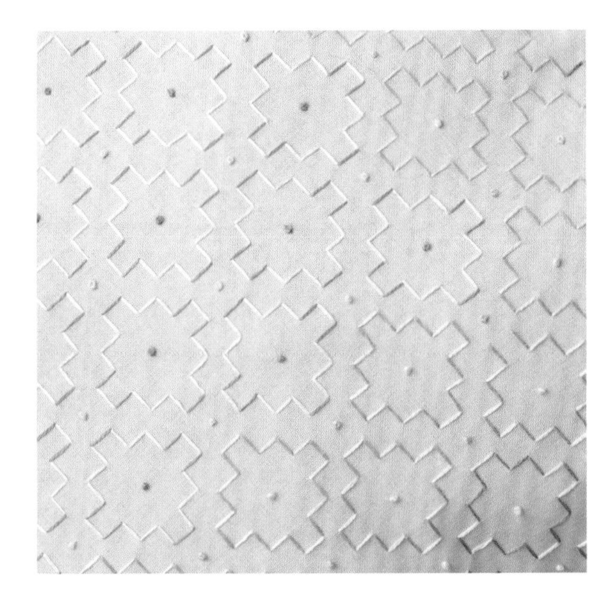

THE TENDERNESS of PEONIES

LEARN TO WORK WITH SILK THREAD

Embroidering with silk thread is a magnificent art which has been around for thousands of years, but which has not been particularly common in Europe due to its cost. You obviously encounter it in fashion, costumes, or on high-end furnishings, but it's not your everyday practice.

TIP

Thanks to new technologies, for several years we have had access to synthetic silks like rayon, which enable us to achieve this embroidery of gentle luster—very different from cotton embroidery. Bear in mind that rayon is a fragile thread. To use it, you need to cut short lengths of thread and moisten it when it begins to fray. But there's nothing mystical about this, so don't be scared—dive right in to this beautiful embroidery filled with poetry.

Materials

9" × 9" (23 × 23cm) square of light blue fabric • DMC Satin Floss: S 351, S 504, S 601, S 606, S 818, S 899, S 959, S 976, S 991 • 6" (15.5cm) embroidery hoop

Stitches

Running stitch • Whipped running stitch • Back stitch • Chain stitch • French knots

DMC number	Color description	Substitution floss
S 351	Satin, Coral	
S 504	Satin, Blue Green	
S 601	Satin, Cranberry Dark	
S 606	Satin, Orange Red	
S 818	Satin, Baby Pink	
S 899	Satin, Rose	
S 959	Satin, Seagreen	
S 976	Satin, Golden Brown	
S 991	Satin, Aquamarine Dark	

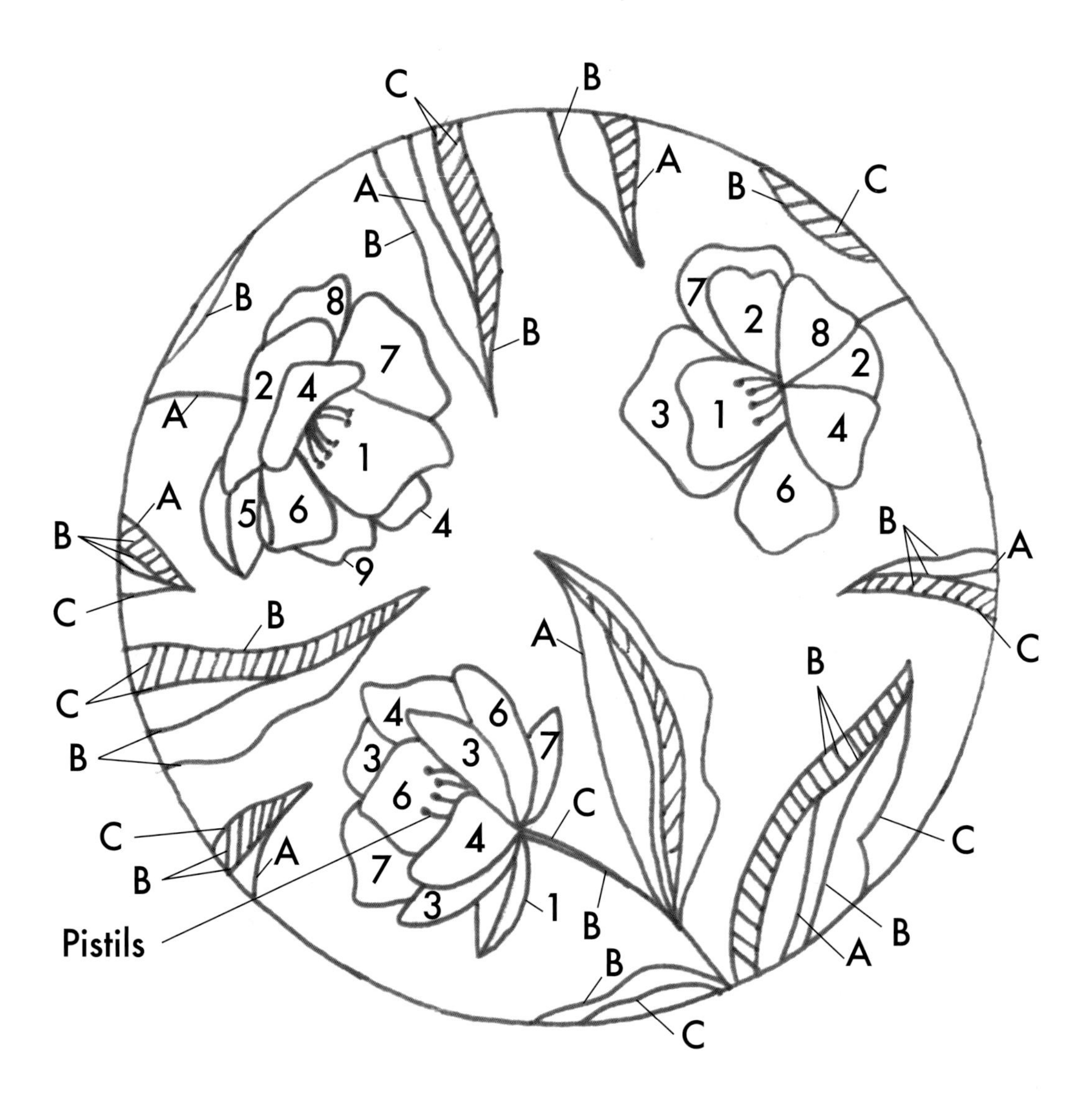
C
B
A
A
B
C
B
B
8
7
2
8
7
2
2
4
B
A
3
1
4
1
6
A
5
6
4
B
B
A
9
C
C
B
A
C
B
C
B
4
6
3
7
3
6
C
3
4
C
C
B
A
7
3
1
B
Pistils
B
A
B
B
C

Actual size

Instructions

1 First transfer your design onto your fabric using an erasable pen, then position it in your embroidery hoop.

2 Embroider the **circle** that surrounds the design using a chain stitch with a single strand of S 959.

3 Once you've finished the circle, use a running stitch with a single strand of S 818 to embroider the 1 **petals**.

4 Next embroider the **2 petals** using a running stitch with a single strand of S 899,

- **3 petals** using a running stitch with a single strand of S 606,
- **4 petals** using a running stitch with a single strand of S 351,
- **5 petals** using a running stitch with a single strand of S 601,
- **6 petals** using a whipped running stitch with a single strand of S 818 (bottom stitch) and a single strand of S 899 (top stitch),
- **7 petals** using a whipped running stitch with a single strand of S 899 (bottom stitch) and a single strand of S 601 (top stitch),
- **8 petals** using a whipped running stitch with a single strand of S 351 (bottom stitch) and a single strand of S 818 (top stitch).

5 Now embroider all the **A lines** using a back stitch with a single strand of S 991,

- all the **B lines** using a back stitch with a single strand of S 959,
- all the **C lines** using a back stitch with a single strand of S 504.

6 Lastly, embroider all the **pistils** with short running stitches using a single strand of S 976, then top each with a small French knot (2 twists around the needle) with the same thread.

7 You can achieve a **pretty finish** with your embroidery hoop by following the pointers given in the last paragraph of Day 5 (pages 48–49).

I hope this project has whetted your appetite for embroidering with this wonderful material in the future.

ENCHANTED COSMOS

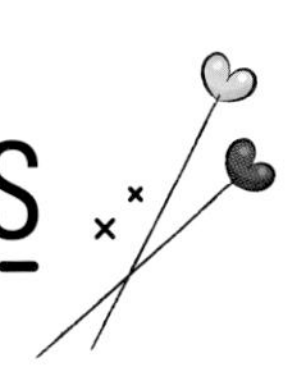

LEARN TO WORK WITHOUT HOOPS OR FRAMES

Today you will learn how to embroider without the support of an embroidery hoop or frame. For your first attempt at freehand embroidery, I offer you this project: embroidering a pretty, poetic lampshade. As it's a relatively rigid object, you can embroider without worrying too much about the support or about your thread tension. This will also allow you to practice the "pre-hole" technique and discover that you can embroider any object that comes into your hands, if the spirit moves you!

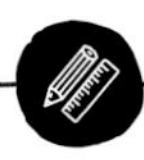

Materials

5.5" × 7" (14 × 18cm) white lampshade • DMC Six-Strand Embroidery Floss: 340, 747, 809, 825, 993, 964, 3041, 3727, 3809, 3852 • A ball head pin

Stitches

Running stitch • Back stitch • Chain stitch • Stem stitch • Lazy daisy • French knots

DMC number	Color description	Substitution floss
340	Blue Violet, Medium	
747	Sky Blue, Very Light	
809	Delft Blue	
825	Blue, Dark	
964	Seagreen, Light	
993	Aquamarine, Very Light	
3041	Antique Violet, Medium	
3727	Antique Mauve, Light	
3809	Turquoise, Very Dark	
3852	Straw, Very Dark	

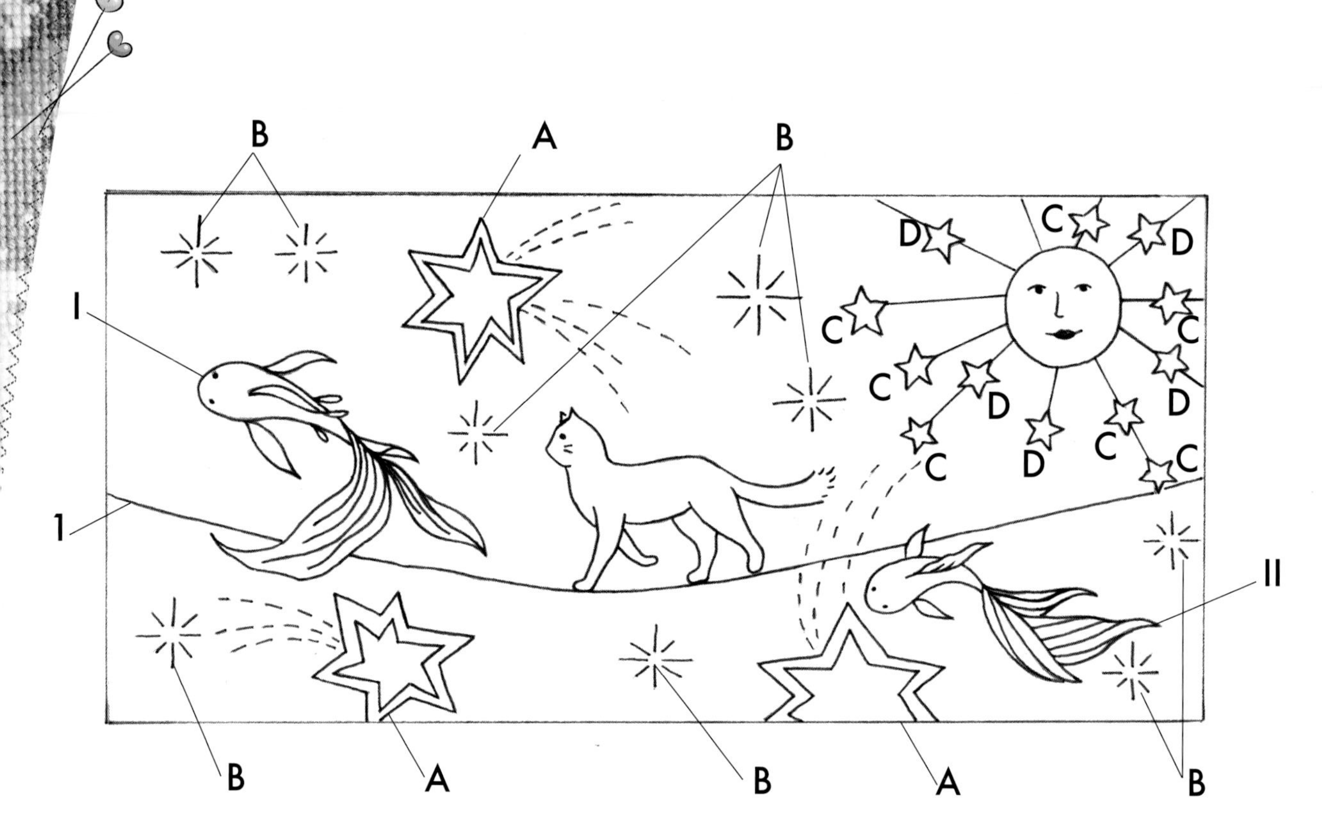

Enlarge 184%

Instructions

1 First transfer your design onto the lampshade with an erasable pen.

2 Grab a ball head pin (or put on your thimble), which will enable you to pre-punch holes in your lampshade before embroidering.
This is a great technique for smoothly embroidering rigid surfaces—and without hurting your fingers. You will need to pre-punch your holes before embroidering each element.

3 Poke holes every ⅛″ (4mm) around the circle of the sun, then embroider it using the chain stitch with a single strand of 3852.

4 Continue embroidering:

- **the rays of the sun** using a back stitch with a double thread of 3852.
- **the sun's face** using a back stitch with a double thread of 3041. Make two French knots for the eyes (2 twists around the needle).
- **stars C** using a back stitch with a double thread of 3727, and stars D in the same way with 340.
- **stars B**. The **horizontal and vertical lines** are embroidered using a back stitch with a double thread of 3852, and the **diagonal** lines are embroidered using a back stitch with a double thread of 3809.

5 Now embroider **stars A:** the **outer star** is embroidered using a back stitch with a double thread of 809, the **inner star** using a chain stitch with a single strand of 340. The trailing lines are embroidered using a running stitch with a double thread of 747. You can scatter stars all around your lampshade.

6 Embroider the **tightrope** using a back stitch with a double thread of 825, then the **cat** using the stem stitch with a double thread of 3041. For the **face**, use a tiny back stitch with a double thread of 825.

7 Next embroider **fish I**. Embroider the body using a back stitch with a double thread of 3809, then use the same thread to make 2 French knots (2 twists around the needle) for the fish's **eyes**.

All the **fins** are embroidered using a back stitch with a double thread: the dorsal fin as well as the largest and smallest tail fins are embroidered with 993, all the other fins are embroidered with 964.

8 For **fish II**, embroider the **body** using a back stitch with a double thread of 3809, then use the same thread to make 2 French knots (2 twists around the needle) for the fish's **eyes**.

All the **fins** are embroidered using a back stitch with a double thread: the dorsal fin and the center tail fin are embroidered with 964, all the other fins are embroidered with 993.

You have now embroidered a pretty lampshade that you can mount for a touch of sweetness and dreaminess. You have also completed a fabulous introduction to freehand embroidery. Bravo, it's a very nice technique to master.

SPRING BONNET

MASTER RAFFIA EMBROIDERY

Raffia is a material we all know: some vague memory from nursery school or as the gardener's best friend, we all have some idea of what this straw thread looks like. You will now discover that it's also a marvelous material for embroidery! Add some flair to a straw bag, embroidering phrases or little animals, spread flowers across a hat, decorate a planter or any other object.

Types of raffia

There are several kinds of raffia: natural raffia (which you can find dyed in all different colors), rayon raffia, which is a synthetic raffia that is wonderfully bright and even, and lastly paper raffia, which likewise comes in all colors and has a matte finish. You can try all three according to your desires and your projects. Raffia thread can be used whole or split in half in order to achieve different thicknesses.

Materials

No. 19 chenille needle • Paper raffia: pale yellow, peach, mauve, navy blue, aqua, and emerald green

Stitches

Back stitch • Satin stitch • Fishbone stitch • Feather stitch • Star stitches • French knots

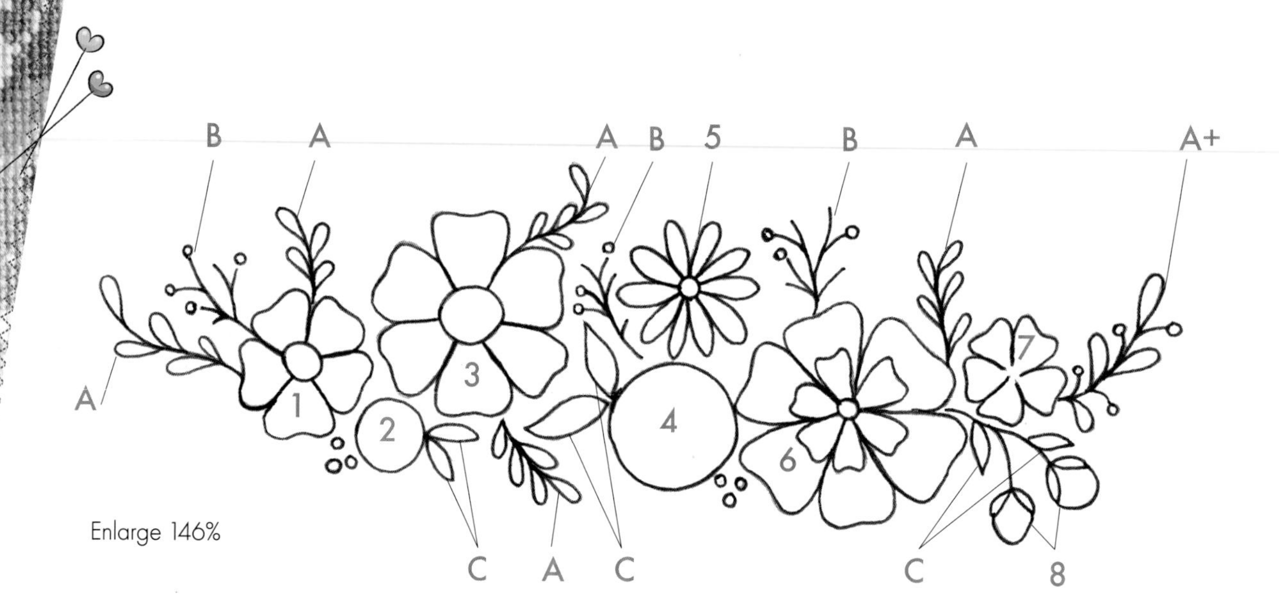

Instructions

1 Begin by **transferring your design**. For this project, I recommend using a strip of water-soluble stabilizer, as it's a flexible material that you can easily apply and remove from the hat. Since it's a straw hat, you will need to remove the water-soluble stabilizer by tearing it away and not by soaking it.

2 Once your design is applied to the hat, you can begin your **embroidery**. For this, cut the end of your raffia at an angle to help it slide through the needle and don't hesitate to stab directly into the straw. Don't forget your thimble, because it's not an easy material to stitch through.

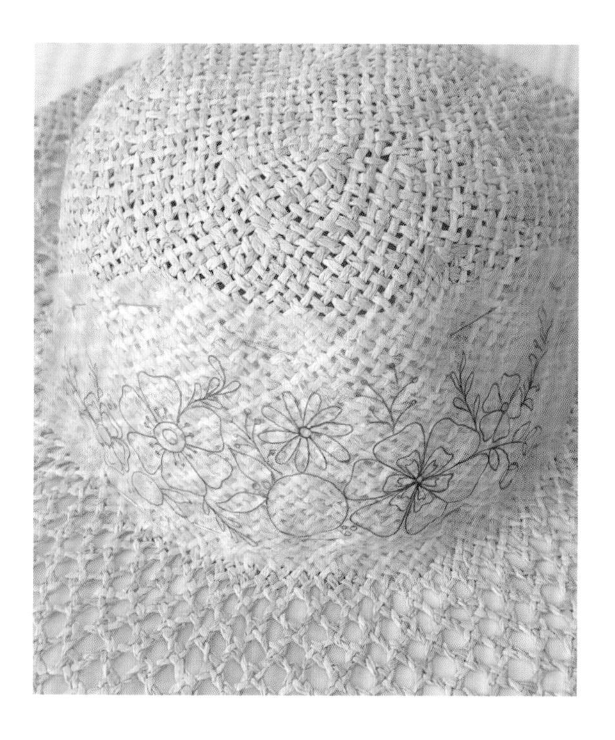

3 Start with **flower 1**: The petals are embroidered using a satin stitch with a strand of pale yellow raffia split in two for a more delicate look. The center of the flower is made using an eyelet stitch with mauve raffia. **Flowers 1, 2, 3, and 4 can be viewed on page 79.**

4 **Flower 2** is embroidered using a satin stitch with a strand of peach raffia.

5 For **flower 3**: The petals are created using a satin stitch with a strand of mauve raffia split in two and the center is created in two stages. The outline is embroidered using a back stitch and the interior using a circular Rhodes stitch with a strand of navy blue raffia split in two.

6 **Flower 4** is created using a satin stitch with a strand of pale yellow split in two.

7 **Flower 5** is created using a variation of the couching stitch. Pull your strand of peach raffia out at the edge of the flower's center, and position it on the petal. Make a couching stitch at the end of the petal with a thread that matches the raffia's color. Fold your raffia over and reinsert your needle where the strand came out. For the center of the flower, create a French knot (1 twist around the needle) with a strand of mauve raffia split in two.

8 The petals of **flower 6** are made using a satin stitch, the outer part with a strand of mauve raffia split in two and the inner part with a strand of pale yellow raffia, also split in two. Embroider the center of the flower using a French knot (1 twist around the needle) using a strand of peach raffia split in two.

9 **Flower 7** is created using a satin stitch, emanating from the center of the flower, with a strand of peach raffia.

10 **The flower 8s** are embroidered using a satin stitch, with a strand of navy blue split in two, and are cradled by two leaves, each embroidered using a running stitch with a strand of aqua raffia split in two. The stems are created using a back stitch with the same thread.

11 The **three little circles** between flowers 1 and 2 are embroidered using a French knot (1 twist around the needle) with a strand of mauve raffia split in two, and those between flowers 4 and 6 are embroidered in the same way with a strand of peach raffia split in two.

12 The **branches in A** are embroidered following the same principle as flower 5, with a strand of emerald green raffia. Pull your strand through at the base of the topmost leaf, hold it in place with a couching stitch at the end of the leaf with a thread of the same color, and fold the strand over. Do not reinsert the strand of raffia back into the hat; bring it down and hold it in place with little couching stitches along the design. For each leaf, make a small couching stitch at the base of the leaf and at the end of the leaf. Fold the strand over, make another couching stitch at the base of the leaf, and repeat.

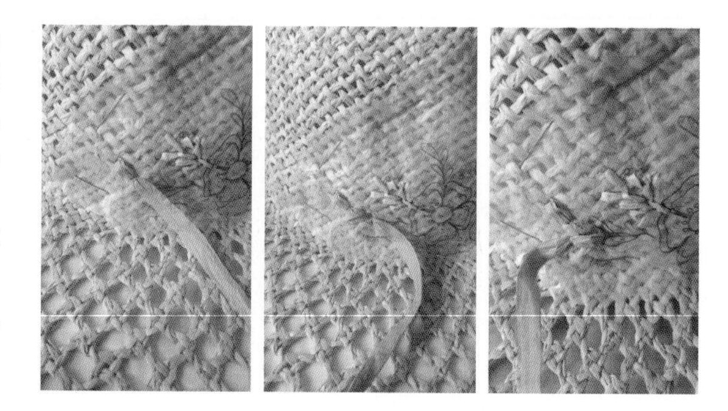

13 The **branches in B** are created using a feather stitch with a strand of aqua raffia split in two. They are topped with little French knots (1 twist around the needle), made with a strand of navy blue split in two.

14 The **leaves in C** are created using a fishbone stitch with strands of raffia split in two. The **leaves for flowers 2 and 8** are stitched with aqua raffia, and the **leaves for flower 4** are stitched with emerald green raffia.

15 **Branch A+** is a mix of branches A and B. The **base** of the branch as well as the **larger leaves** are stitched like branch A, the **smaller branches** topped with buds are embroidered using a running stitch with a strand of aqua raffia split in two, and the buds are embroidered using a French knot (1 twist around the needle) with a strand of navy blue raffia split in two.

16 You can now gently remove your water-soluble stabilizer, using tweezers for any stubborn bits that remain.

Enjoy your hat all summer long—you've earned it!

Grace & Mila

MY WINTER GARDEN

LEARN TO EMBROIDER A CARDIGAN WITH YARN

If your sweaters lack a little magic, if you don't know what to do with the ends of your yarn skeins, or if you're simply looking for some new ideas for embroidery, then smile—this lesson was made just for you!

As always, the key is to master your thread tension. You will need a good yarn needle or a large chenille needle and several strands of colored yarn. You can, of course, mix your yarns, alternate between materials, and combine mohair with cotton: the possibilities are endless! For our little introduction, and to make things easier, I'm offering you a project embroidered with Tapestry yarn, but you are free to use whatever you like.

For this embroidery, you will need to hold your cardigan with one hand and stitch with the other. Your movements should be slow and gentle so as not to create tension which could spoil your work. If a movement is a little too abrupt, you can ease the tension in your stitches by gently pulling on your yarn.

Try to hide the beginnings and ends of your thread within the knit of your fabric, but if the knit is too loose and this is not possible, try to make sturdy little knots using the your cardigan's material.

Materials

A white cardigan • A yarn needle or a no. 18 chenille needle • DMC Diamant: D3821 • DMC Tapestry Wool: 7010, 7404, 7541, 7920

Stitches

Stem stitch • Satin stitch • Fishbone stitch • Lazy daisy • French knots

DMC number	Color description	Substitution floss
D3821	Light Gold	
7010	Strawberry Chew	
7404	Poplar	
7541	Pond Green	
7920	Blood Orange	

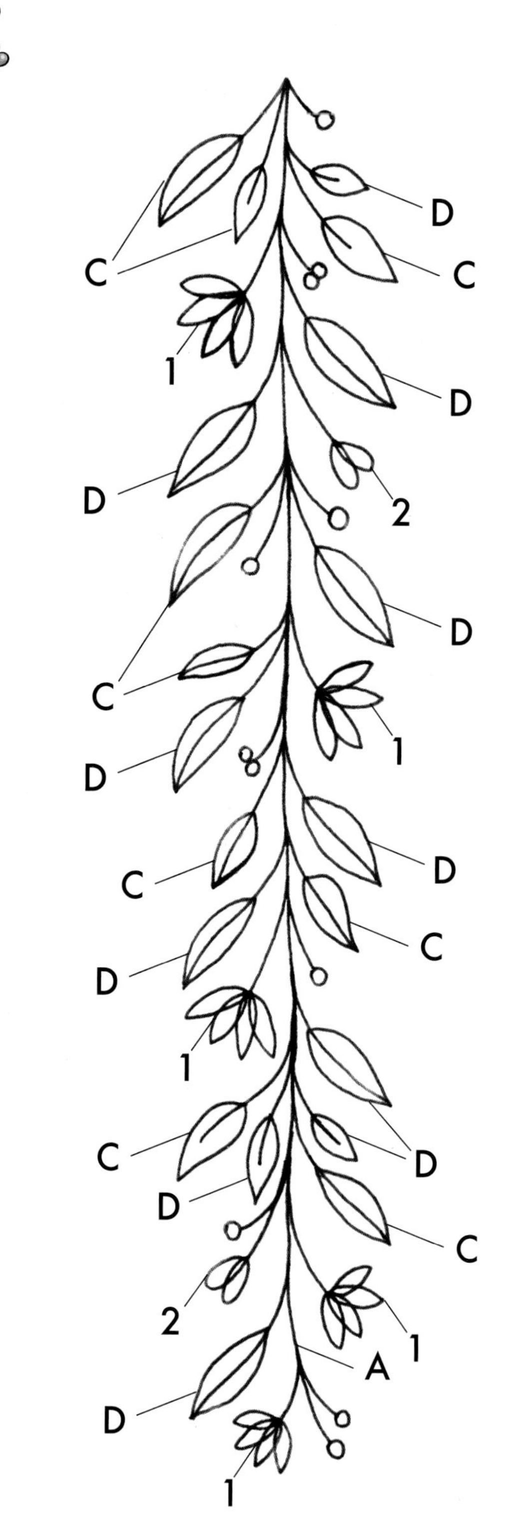
D
C
C
1
D
D
2
D
C
1
D
D
C
C
D
1
C
D
D
C
2
1
A
D
1

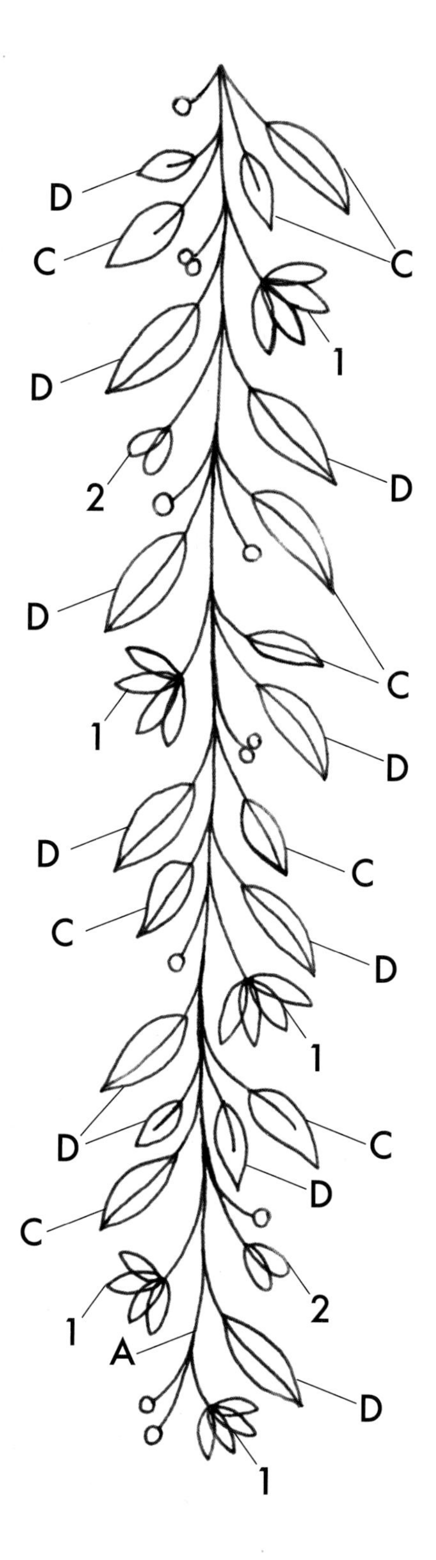
D
C
C
1
D
D
2
D
C
1
D
D
C
C
D
1
D
C
D
C
2
1
A
D
1

Enlarge 147%

Instructions

1 Begin by **transferring your designs** onto each side of your cardigan. To do this, you can use an erasable pen or, if it's too difficult to see the design through the fabric in order to trace, you can also transfer the design to some water-soluble stabilizer and pin it to your sweater. Position each design so that they line up well with the cardigan's shoulders and buttonholes.

This project is **embroidered freehand**. But watch out—this time your ground fabric is completely soft, so you must be extra careful with your thread tension! This is the last project in this book that will be embroidered in this way and it's a technique that you will have completely mastered by the end of today.

Every strand of yarn will be doubled with a strand of Diamant D3821 thread.

2 You can now embroider all the **stems** starting with the central stems in A, using the stem stitch with a strand of 7404 yarn (along with a strand of D3821 thread).

3 Next embroider:

- **flowers 1** using a satin stitch with a strand of 7010 (along with a strand of D3821).
- **flowers 2** using the lazy daisy stitch with a strand of 7010 (along with a strand of D3821).

4 Now embroider all the **little balls** using French knots with a strand of 7920 (along with a strand of D3821), twisting only once around the needle.

5 Continue with:

- **leaves C** using the fishbone stitch with a strand of 7404 (along with a strand of D3821).
- **leaves D** in the same way, but with a strand of 7920 (along with a strand of D3821).

6 If you have transferred your design with a marker, give the cardigan a quick steam with your iron, and if you have used water-soluble stabilizer, gently tear it away, holding on with one hand so as not to pull too hard on your stitches.

Over the course of the last three days, you have learned to embroider freehand on different materials, so you should have perfectly mastered this technique! You can wear your cardigan with pride, and why not embroider every sweater in your wardrobe...

DMC
HAPPY
CHENILLE

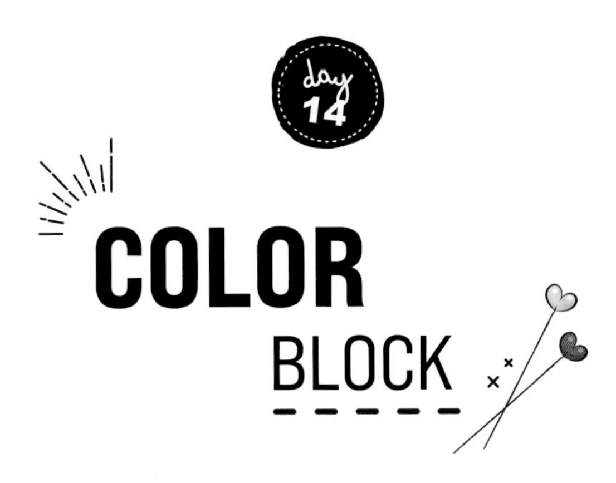

COLOR BLOCK

MASTER EMBROIDERING WITH CHENILLE

Let's build on our momentum and continue learning about the different kinds of thread we can use in our embroidery. Today, we're going to try out chenille. This is a furry thread that is often used in high fashion, traditionally made of silk, which gives it quality that is both velvety and shimmery.

Silk chenille is amazing but it is quite costly. You can find it from Au Ver à Soie. Fortunately for us, There are many lines of chenille yarn that allow you to achieve very nice results.

For this project, I present to you some playful and colorful embroidery to decorate your walls with good cheer.

You can use a satin stitch with chenille, if the weave of your fabric is particularly loose. You can also pre-punch your holes using an awl to allow your chenille to pass through without fraying. However, the simplest method is to use a couching stitch with a thread of the same color.

There are needles called "chenille" needles (which have a very large eye and are very sharp). They allow you to thread your needle and penetrate the fabric with ease.

Materials

One 10" (26cm) and one 12" (30cm) embroidery hoop • 12" × 12" (30 × 30cm) royal blue fabric square • Chenille yarn in melon, medium yellow, pale mint, aquamarine, turquoise, lilac, medium blue • No. 18 chenille needle

Stitches

Couching stitch • French knots

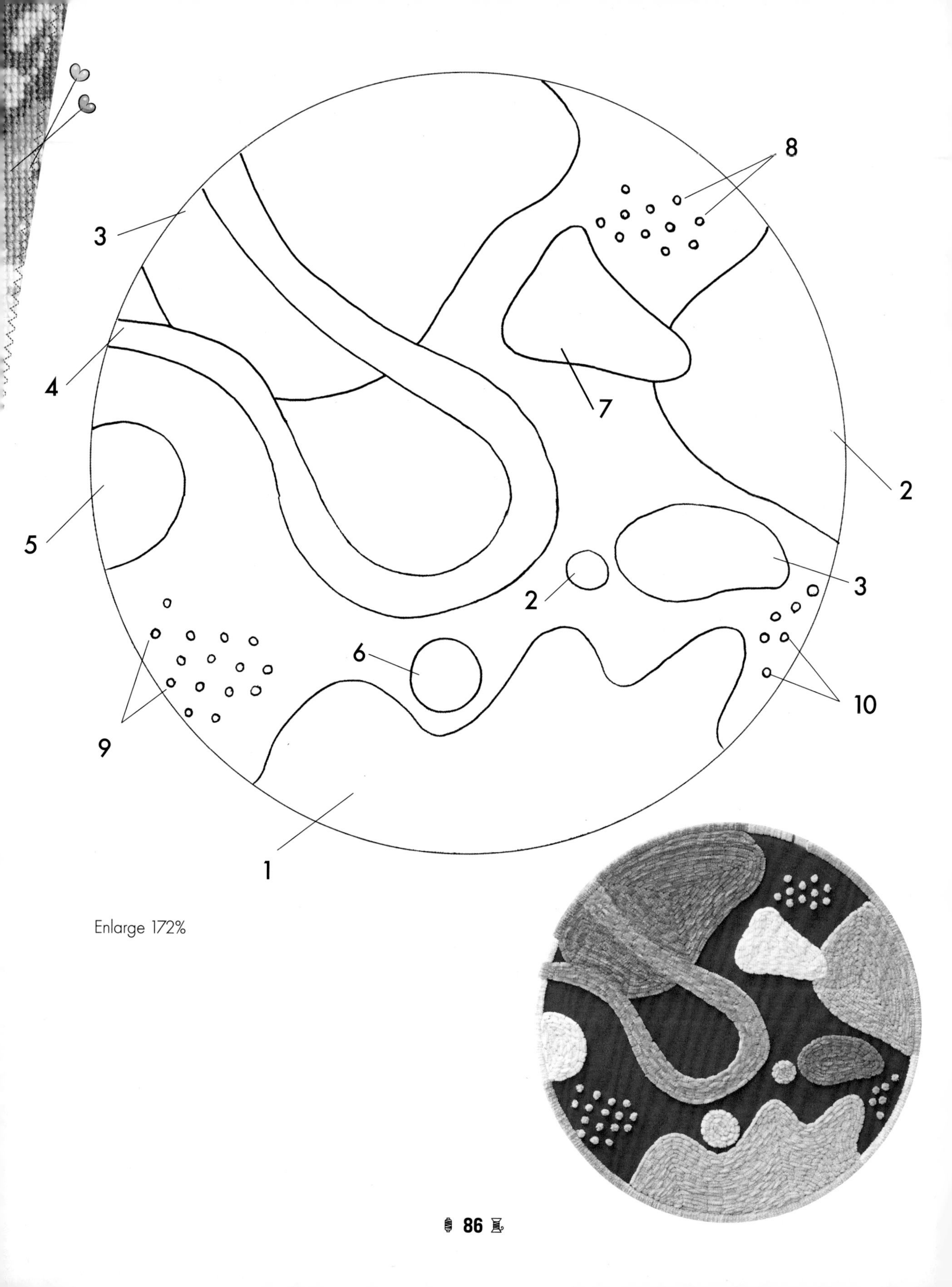

Enlarge 172%

Instructions

1 Transfer your design then position your fabric in the 12″ (30cm) embroidery hoop.

2 All of the large areas of color are embroidered using a couching stitch and the little balls are embroidered using French knots (1 twist around the needle).

3 Embroider the colored areas according to the following information (refer to the diagram opposite):

- **section 1**: Medium blue
- **section 2s**: Aquamarine
- **section 3s**: Lilac
- **section 4**: Melon
- **section 5**: Pale mint
- **section 6**: Turquoise
- **section 7**: Medium yellow
- **dot 8s**: Medium blue
- **dot 9s**: Aquamarine
- **dot 10s**: Melon

Assembly

1 Once your embroidery is complete, place your work in the 10″ (26cm) embroidery hoop and using your erasable pen, make little marks everywhere your colored areas touch the rim of your hoop.

2 Once you've marked the outer circle of your embroidery hoop, disassemble it.

Wrap each section between your marks with the yarn that corresponds to the colored area. To do this, glue the end of the yarn ¼″ (0.5cm) from the mark (in the space between the marks). Once the glue has set, position your yarn on the outside of your mark and wrap your embroidery hoop until you reach the second mark.

3 Thread your needle with the yarn and bury it under the yarn wrapped around the hoop, then cut your yarn as close as you can. Do the same for each section.

4 Now you can fill the holes that remain in your embroidery hoop with whichever colors you like, or you can follow the example in the photos.

Stages of assemblyage

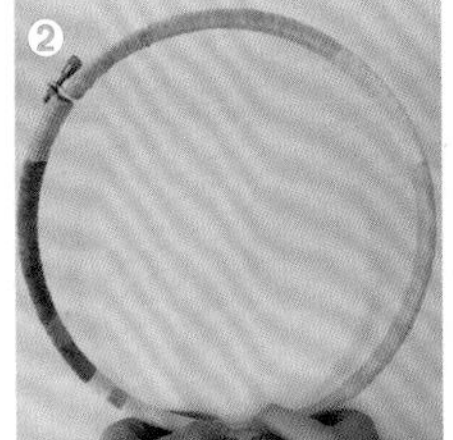

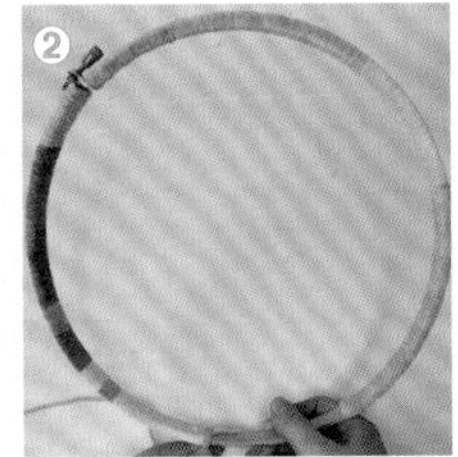

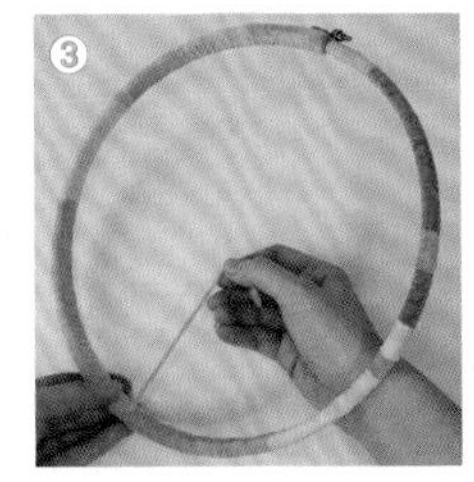

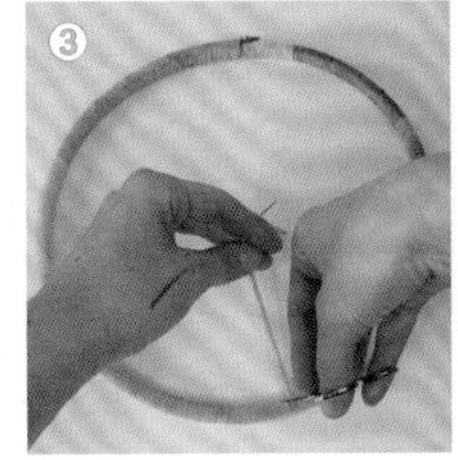

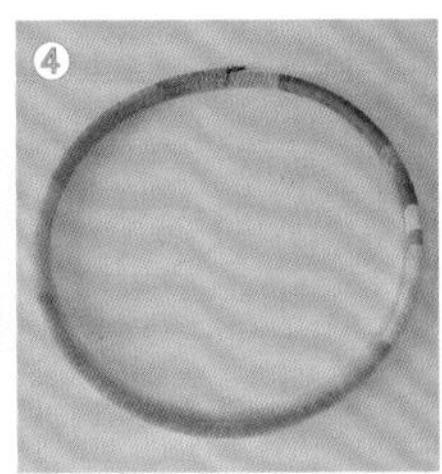

This lesson is a little introduction to chenille, a very beautiful thread when mixed with other materials like beads and sequins. Now it's up to you to experiment with this technique as much as you like!

THE TIME of FLOWERS

MASTER RIBBON EMBROIDERY

Today we will look at the art of ribbon embroidery through a very simple project that mixes traditional embroidery techniques with certain techniques specific to embroidering with ribbons.
Ribbon embroidery does indeed have its own stitches and its own guidelines, but it's absolutely possible to embroider with ribbons using what you've already learned. Use a needle with a large eye and a pointed tip, cut the end of your ribbon at an angle, and slide it into your needle.

There are ribbons made of organza, polyester, cotton, and silk. They come in all varieties, all colors, all sizes, and they can be shiny, satin, velvety, sheer, matte, etc. You can even paint your own ribbons.

Materials

Emerald green fabric, 22″ × 12″ (55 × 30cm) • Dark blue gingham fabric, 22″ × 12″ (55 × 30cm) •No. 5 needle • Silk ribbons, 4mm: golden yellow, steel blue, orchid pink, and cream • DMC Six-Strand Embroidery Floss: 782, 992, and 993

For assembly

Heavy nylon thread • Faceted bi-cone beads in forest green and pale pink • Round beads in clear and pale purple • 2 golden jump rings

Stitches

Lazy daisy • French knots • Woven wheel stitch • Stem stitch • Rose stitch (ribbon technique) • Leaf stitch (ribbon technique) • Petal stitch (ribbon technique)

DMC number	Color description	Substitution floss
782	Topaz, Dark	
992	Aquamarine, Light	
993	Aquamarine, Very Light	

Instructions

1 Begin by practicing our three new ribbon stitching techniques on a little piece of fabric.

- **Leaf stitch** (also known as the **ribbon stitch**)

1. Pull your ribbon through to the right side of your fabric.

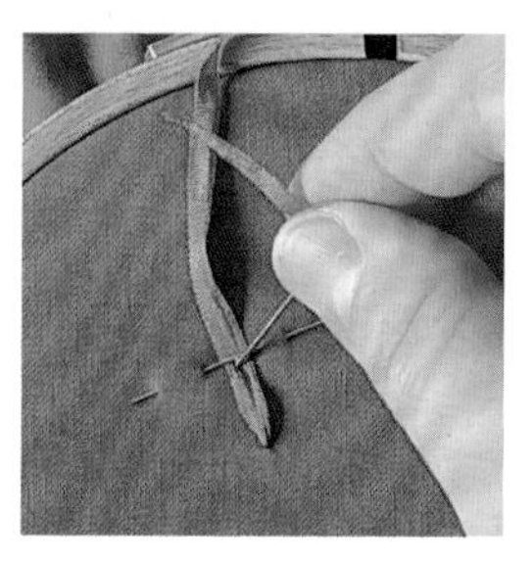

2. Hold your ribbon in place with a small pin.

3. Reinsert your needle into the ribbon just below the pin and pull your needle through on the back of your fabric. Knot the ribbon and remove the pin.

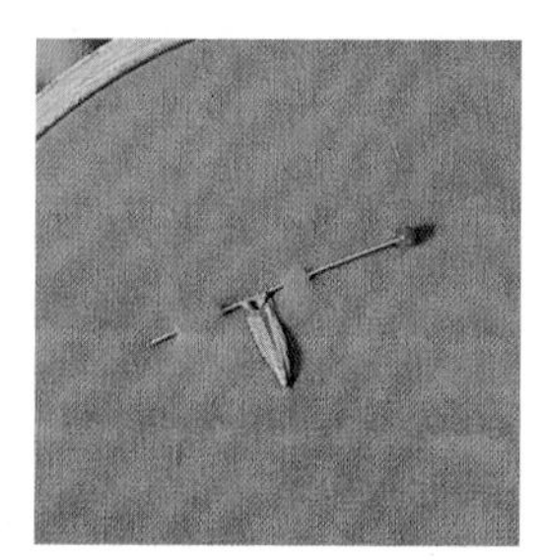

- **Petal stitch**

1. Pull your ribbon through to the right side of your fabric.
2. Make a small couching stitch to hold your ribbon ½″ (1 cm) from where your ribbon comes out.

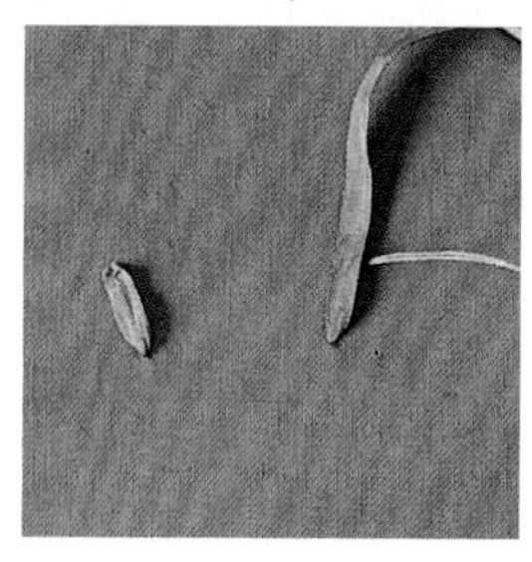

3. Reinsert your needle in the same place the ribbon comes out and pull it through to the back of the fabric.

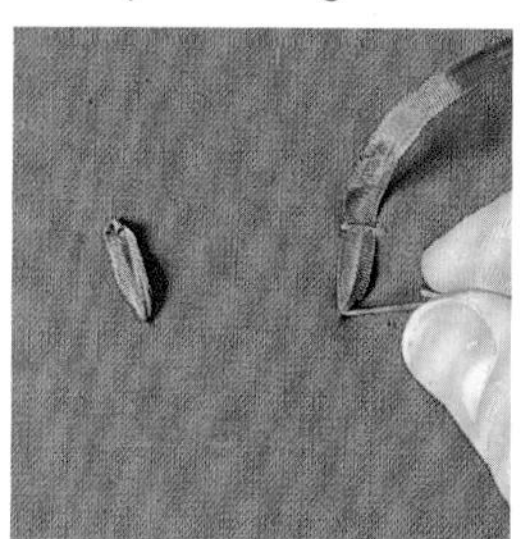

• **Rose stitch** (also known as the **folded stitch**)

1. Pull your ribbon through to the right side of your fabric.
2. Hold your ribbon in place and twist it around the needle, as you would for a French knot.

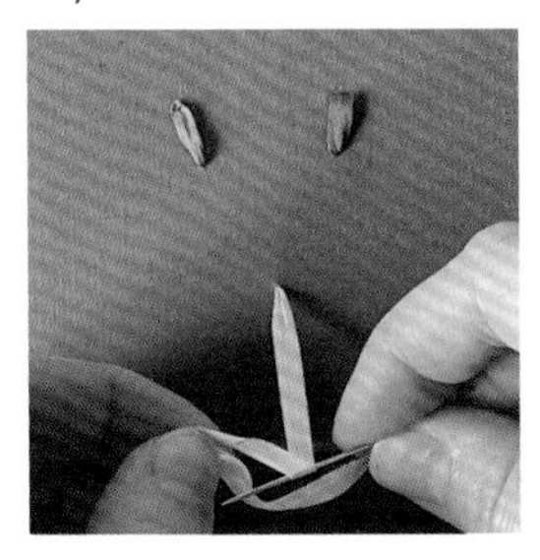

3. Holding your loop on the needle, stick the needle through the center of the ribbon 4 times in the space between the fabric and your loop (⅛″ or 4mm of space between these points).

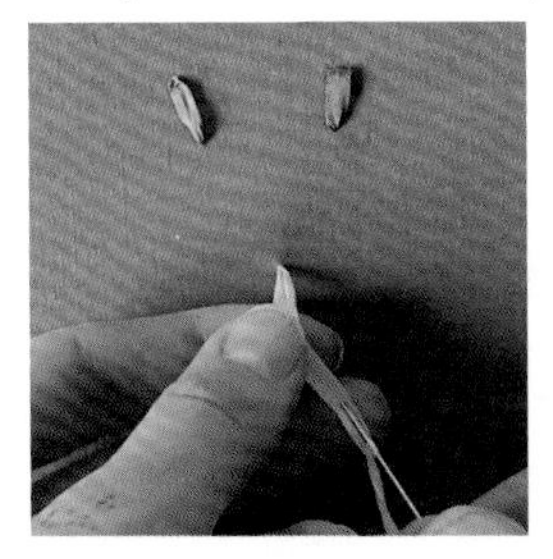

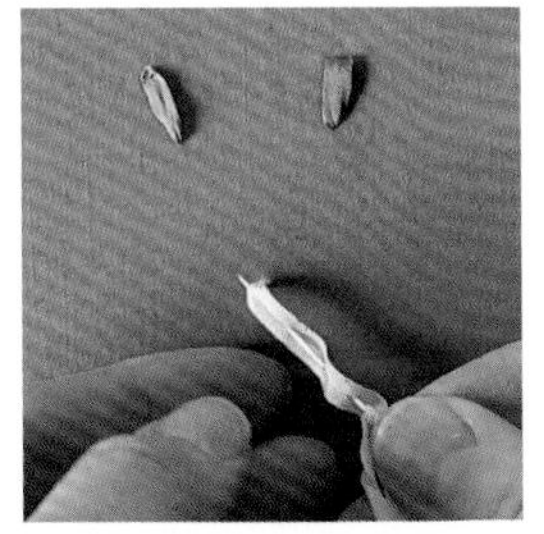

4. Reinsert your needle next to where the ribbon comes out of the fabric and pull your ribbon through to the back of the fabric. Gently adjust your folds so they are staggered.

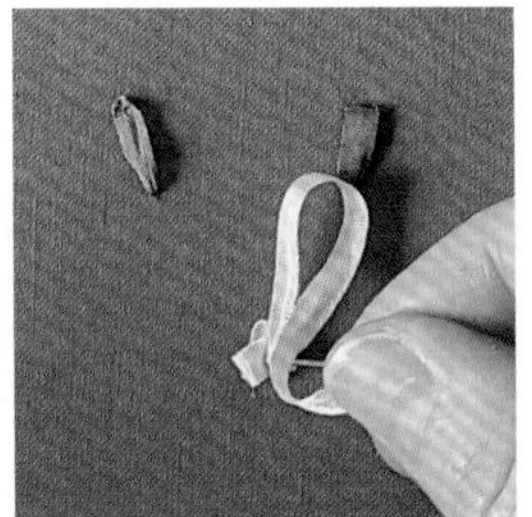

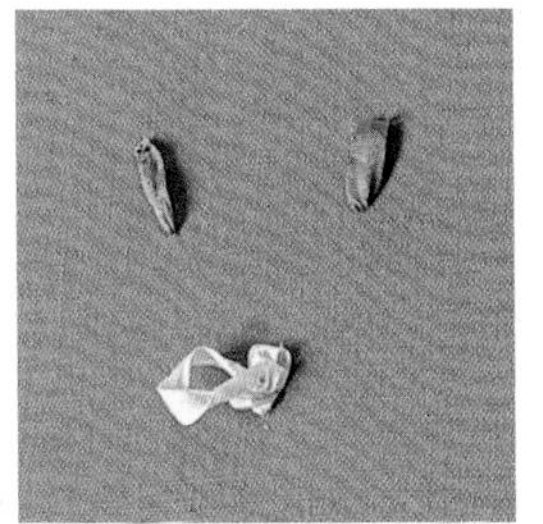

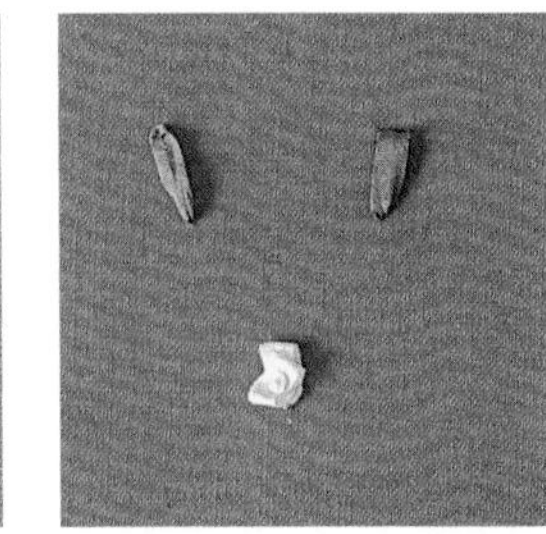

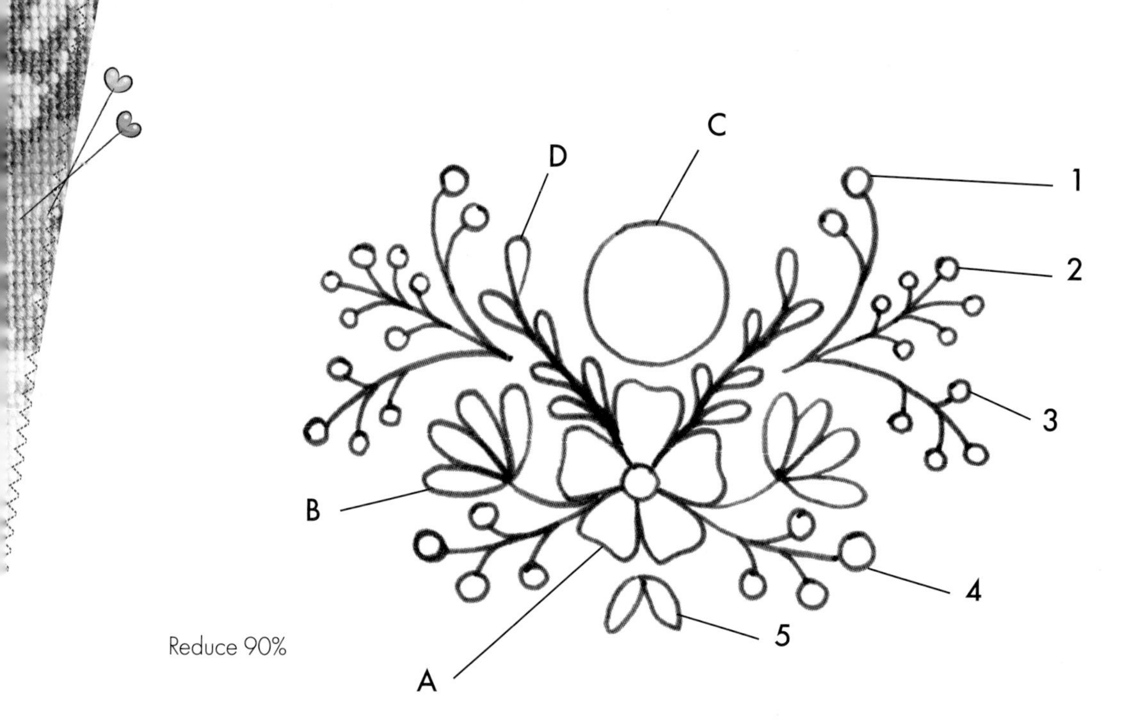

Reduce 90%

2 Trace a 10″ × 16″ (25 × 40cm) rectangle on your green fabric and position your design so that the number 5 flower is against the shortest side of the rectangle. The rounded bottom edge of the embroidery is the shape of the front flap of the bag.
Traditionally in ribbon embroidery, there is a specific method for creating a knot at the end of the ribbon, but for us, since the ribbons we're using are very fine and fragile, we'll make a little knot at the end, just like how you knot your thread.

3 Begin by embroidering **flower A** using the leaf stitch (ribbon stitch), covering the petal design with several stitches, with the cream ribbon. The center of the flower is made up of 3 French knots (1 twist around the needle) with steel blue ribbon.

4 Next embroider **flower B** and its mirror image using the petal stitch with the golden yellow ribbon, then embroider the flower's stem using the stem stitch with a double thread of floss 993. Continue with **flower C** using the woven wheel stitch with the orchid pink ribbon, then **branch D** and its mirror image, first using the stem stitch with a double thread of floss 992, then embroidering the **leaves** using the leaf stitch (ribbon stitch) with the steel blue ribbon.

5 Now embroider **flowered branches 1, 2, and 3** (and their mirror images), beginning with the stems, using the stem stitch with a double thread: **stems 1 and 2** are embroidered with floss 993 and **stem 3** with 992. The **flower 1s** are embroidered using the rose stitch (folded stitch) with the golden yellow ribbon, **flower 2s** using French knots with the cream ribbon (1 twist around the needle), and **flower 3s** are also embroidered using French knots with orchid pink ribbon (1 twist around the needle).

6 Next embroider the **flower 4s** and their mirror images, beginning with the stem using the stem stitch with a double thread of floss 992, then embroider the flowers using the rose stitch (folded stitch) with stell blue ribbon. To finish, make the two lazy daisy petals in **5** with orchid pink ribbon.

Assembly

1 Cut your fabric ½″ (1cm) from the outline of your rectangle creating a rounded flap, then cut this same shape from your lining fabric and batting.

2 Place the batting against the reverse side of your embroidered fabric, then place the right side of your embroidered fabric against the right side of the lining. Pin all layers together.

3 Sew all around the curved flap, following the edge of the curve ½″ (1 cm) from the edge, then notch the curve. Sew along the other end, along the shortest straight side, also ½″ (1 cm) from the edge of the fabric. (Do not sew the straight sides.)

Trim your seams, cutting out the extra batting.

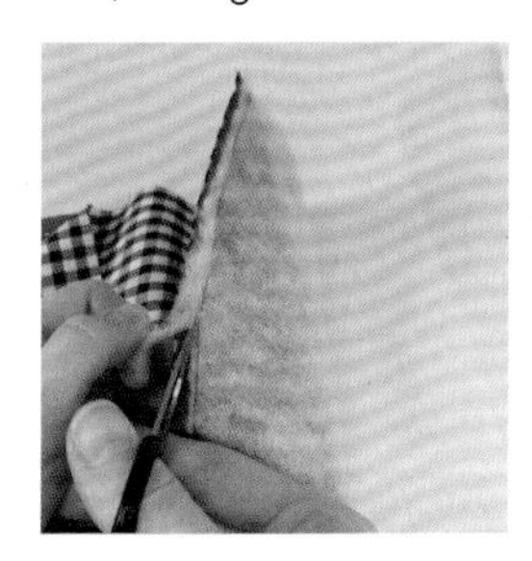

4 Fold your work so that your lining rectangles are together and your green rectangles are also together, keeping the flap in the middle. Sew all around this new rectangle (without sewing the flap), leaving an opening of an inch or two (a few centimeters) in the lining. Once you've finished sewing, turn your work right side out, close the little opening, place the lining in the purse, and iron.

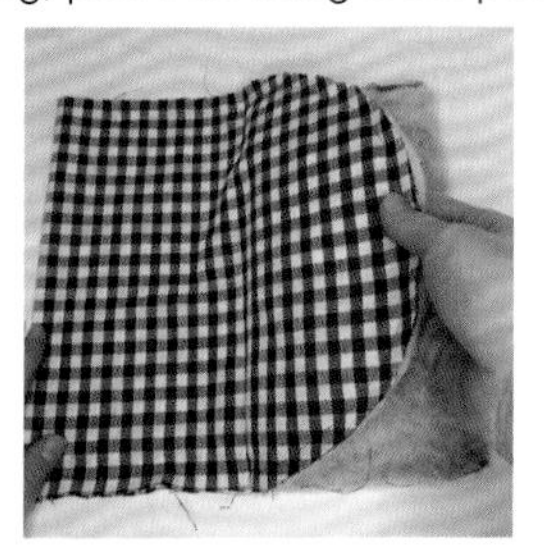

5 Take a double thread of the nylon string and cut it to your desired length for the strap, adding a little extra for assembly. String your beads, alternating between round beads and bi-cone beads.

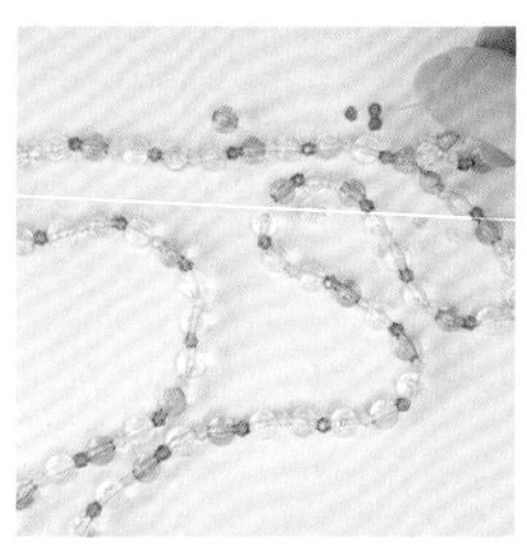

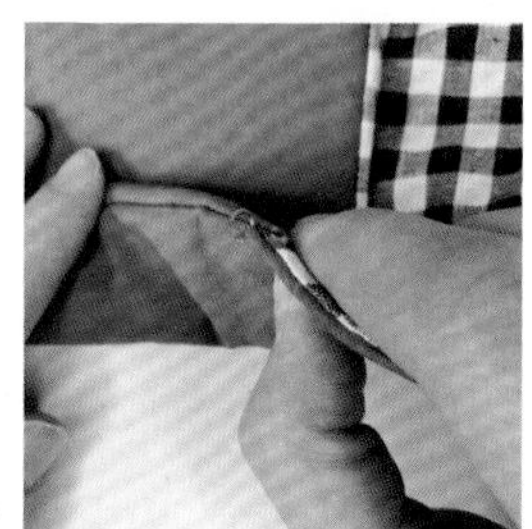

6 Grab your jump rings and open them with pliers. Still using the pliers, place the rings on each side of the bag, sliding them through the stitching and the fabric. Close the ring and attach the strap with a double knot. Once your knot is secure, thread the nylon string back through the last 10 beads (to strengthen the attachment), then cut the end.

LEARN TO WORK WITH METALLIC THREAD

It's got to sparkle! Head to toe, embroidered in metallic thread, challenge accepted. I'm asking you to lay your cards on the table and embroider a tote bag with shimmery shiny threads. This lesson will allow you to master the different kinds of metallic thread as well as 100% lurex threads. This is very good practice that will let you experience the different qualities of each type of thread. Pay attention to your tension, cut short lengths of thread, don't choose too fine a needle, wet your thread if you need to, and away we go!

Materials

Natural cotton tote bag • DMC Diamant: D168, D225, D316 • DMC Mouliné Light Effects: E677, E967, E3747 • DMC Étoile: C519, C550, C554, C603, C798, C816, C820, C823, C900 • DMC Six-Strand Embroidery Floss: 320, 3816, 3817

Stitches

Running stitch • Back stitch • Couching stitch • Chain stitch • Stem stitch • Satin stitch • Fishbone stitch • Star stitch • Lazy daisy • French knots

DMC number	Color description	Substitution floss
E677	Metallic, White Gold	
E967	Metallic, Soft Peach	
E3747	Metallic, Sky Blue	
C519	Étoile, Sky Blue	
C550	Étoile, Violet, Very Dark	
C554	Étoile, Violet, Light	
C603	Étoile, Cranberry	
C798	Étoile, Delft Blue, Dark	
C816	Étoile, Garnet	
C820	Étoile, Royal Blue, Very Dark	
C823	Étoile, Blue, Dark	
C900	Étoile, Burnt Orange, Dark	
320	Pistachio Green, Medium	
3816	Celadon Green	
3817	Celadon Green, Light	

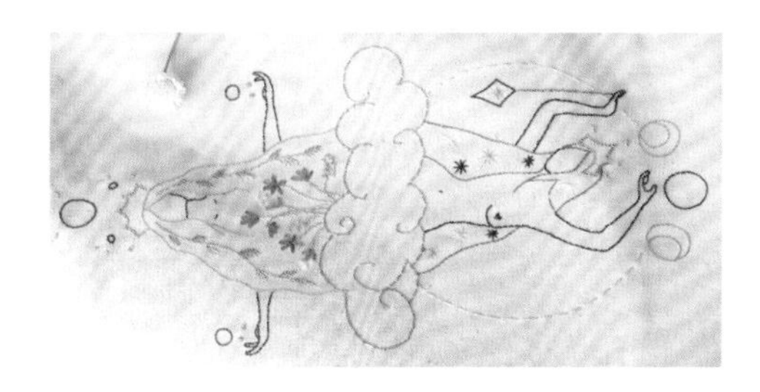

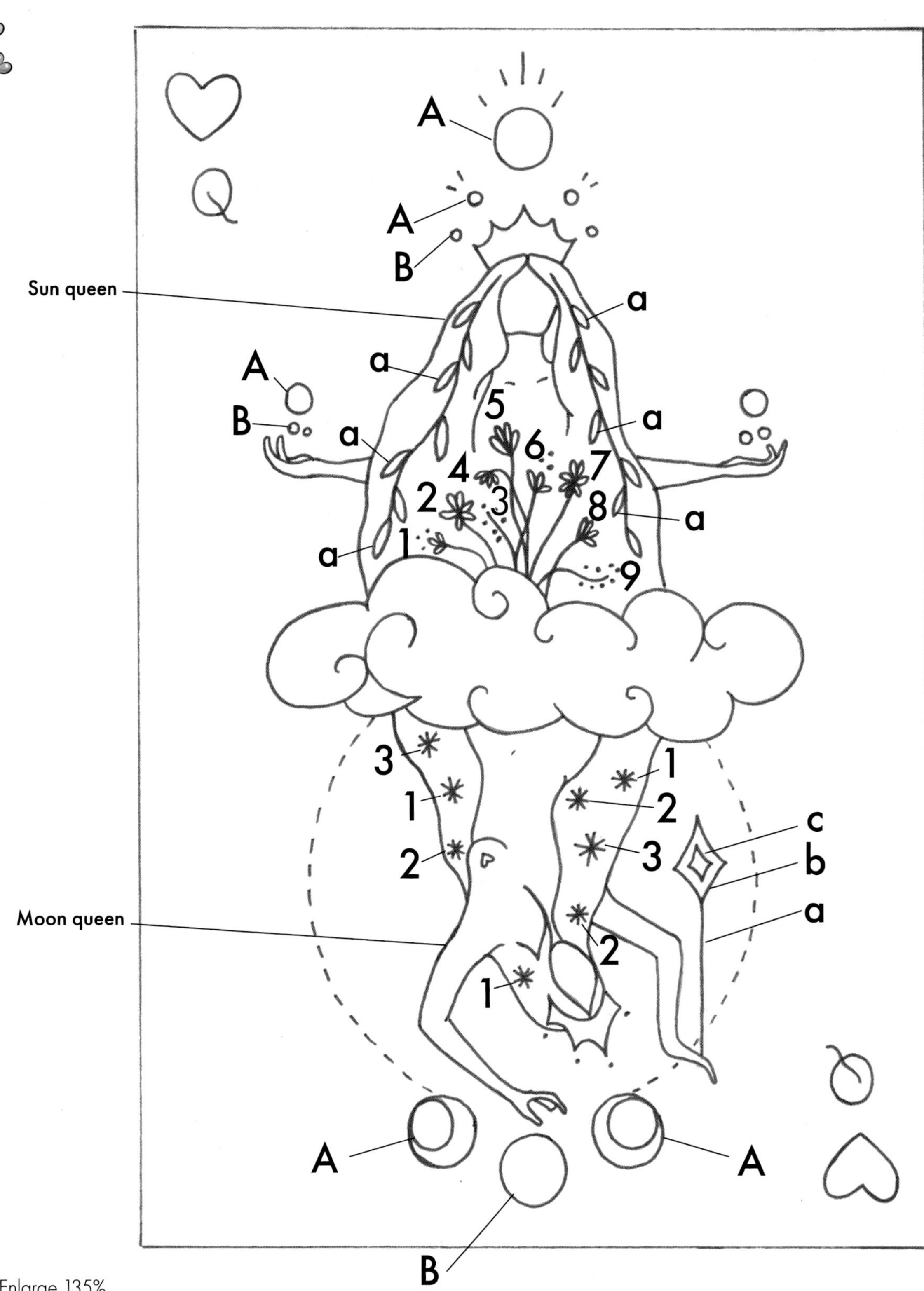
A
A
B
Sun queen
a
A
a
B
5
a
a
6
7
4
2
3
8
a
a
1
9
3
1
1
2
2
3
c
b
a
2
Moon queen
2
1
A
A
B

Enlarge 135%

Instructions

1 Start by **transferring the design** to the center of the tote, then **position your embroidery hoop**. You can undo the seams of the tote to get your fabric flat.

2 Paying close attention to your thread tension, embroider the **frame** of the tarot card using the chain stitch, with a single strand of D316.
If the metallic threads make maintaining tension difficult, you can always use the damp cloth ironing technique when you've completed your embroidery.
With the same thread, embroider the **two Qs** using a back stitch.

3 Next embroider the **two big hearts** using a back stitch to create the outline with a double thread of C816, then with the same thread, fill the interior of the hearts with little French knots (2 twists around the needle).

4 Now embroider the queens' **bodies** using a back stitch with a double thread of C823. You can also embroider the heart within the moon queen using a satin stitch with a double thread of C816.

5 Next embroider the queens' **hair** using the chain stitch with a single strand. Use C554 for the sun queen and C798 for the moon queen. Then embroider the halo around the moon queen using a running stitch with a double thread of D168.

6 Now embroider the **two crowns** using the chain stitch with a single strand of 225. With the same thread, you can also make the 4 French knots above the moon queen's crown (2 twists around the needle).

7 Embroider the **stems in the sun queen's hair** using the stem stitch with a double thread of 3816. Then embroider the **leaves** using the fishbone stitch with a double thread, the leaves marked "a" are embroidered with E677 and the unmarked leaves with 320.

8 Continue with the **stars in the moon queen's hair** using the Rhodes (star) stitch with a double thread: stars 1 with E3747, stars 2 with C820, and stars 3 with C519.

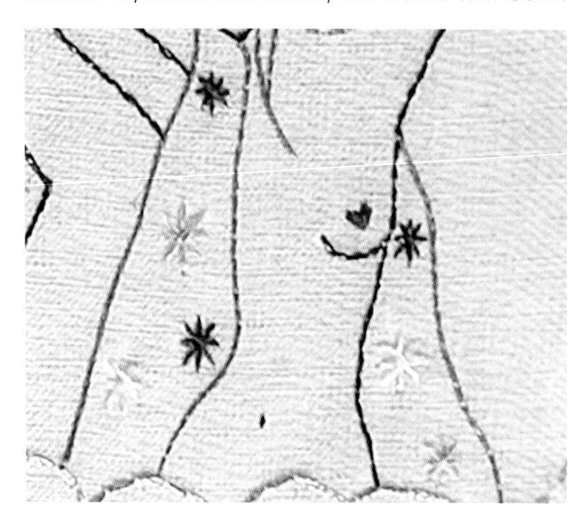

9 Embroider the **cloud** using a couching stitch with a double strand of D225 for the bottom thread.

For the **sun queen's half of the cloud**, use a single strand of D316 for the couching thread.
For the **moon queen's half of the cloud**, use a single strand of 3747 for the couching thread.

10 Next embroider the **sun queen's suns**.

The A suns are embroidered using the chain stitch with a single strand of C550, the rays with a double thread of E677.
The B suns are embroidered using French nots with a double thread of E677 (2 twists around the needle).

11 Embroider the **moon queen's moons** using the chain stitch with a single strand. The A moons are embroidered with C554 and the B moon with C550.

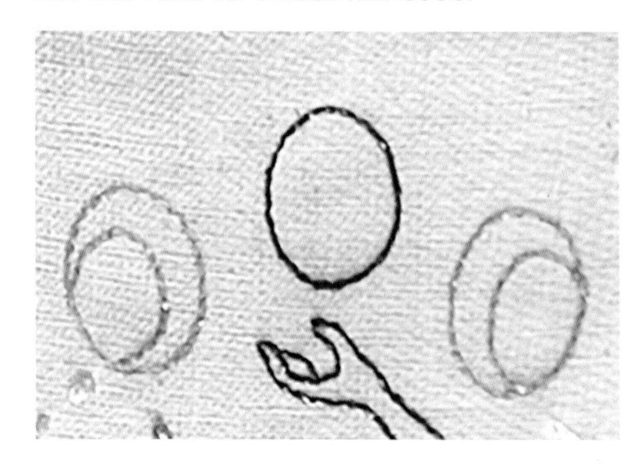

12 Continue with the sun queen's bouquet of flowers. All the stems are embroidered using the stem stitch with a double thread.

Flower 1: Embroider the stem with 3817, then embroider the flower using three lazy daisy stitches with a double thread of C603, and finally embroider three French knots with a double thread of E967 above the petals.

Flower 2: Embroider the stem with 3816, then embroider the flower using the lazy daisy stitch with a double thread, alternating between C603 and C900.

Flower 3: Embroider the stem with 3817, then make French knots with a double thread of E677 to create the flower.

Flowers 4 and 8: Embroider the stem with 3816, then make four lazy daisy stitches with a double strand of C900.

Flowers 5 and 7: Embroider the stem with 3817, then embroider the flower using the lazy daisy stitch with a double thread, alternating between C603 and C900.

Flower 6: Embroider the stem with 3816, then embroider the flower using three lazy daisy stitches with a double thread of C603, and finally embroider three French knots with a double strand of E967 above the petals.

Flower 9: Embroider the stem with 3816, then make French knots with a double strand of E677 to create the flower.

13 Lastly, finish by embroidering the **moon queen's amulet**: the **cord (a)** is embroidered using the stem stitch with a double thread of C798, the **pendant (b)** is embroidered using the chain stitch with a single strand of C820, and the **little star (c)** is embroidered using the Rhodes (star) stitch with a double thread of C519.

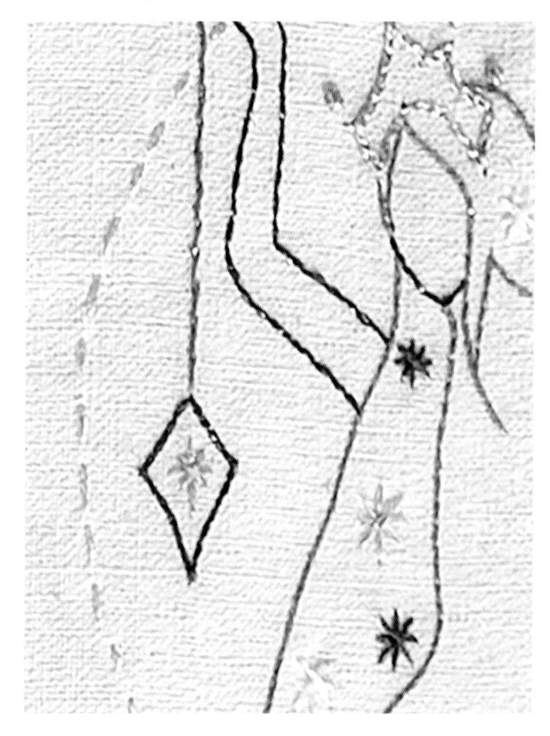

You now have a good understanding of embroidering with metallic thread! Bravo, it's been a successful day!

BOHEMIAN

MIRROR

GET COMFORTABLE EMBROIDERING WITH THREE STRANDS, UNDERSTAND HOW TO GAUGE YOUR THREAD TENSION, LEARN TO PREPARE YOUR EMBROIDERY

On this beautiful seventeenth day, let's embroider an enchanting frame for a mirror, practicing your embroidery hand a little differently from what we've done up to now. It's an interesting exercise to change thread types or, as in this case, change thread thicknesses, as it forces you to concentrate on the fluidity of your movements. The thread will not slide through the fabric as it has before, and with a stitch like the chain stitch, you have to pay close attention not to pull too hard on your thread. Embroidering with more strands enables you to achieve a more dimensional finish and bolder colors. To the needles!

Materials

2 squares 16˝ × 16˝ (40 × 40cm) of aqua fabric • Large 10˝ embroidery hoop or frame • No. 6 needle • DMC Six-Strand Embroidery Floss: 309, 352, 517, 964, 3727, 3750, 3760, 3848

For the assembly

A round mirror, 8˝ (20cm) in diameter • A 16˝ × 16˝ (40 × 40cm) square of batting • A ring hanger • 3 squares 16˝ × 16˝ (40 × 40cm) of recycled cardboard • Strong glue (gel super glue) Double-sided tape • Sewing clips or clothespins

Stitches

Chain stitch • French knots • Star stitches • Tuft couching

DMC number	Color description	Substitution floss
309	Rose, Dark	
352	Coral, Light	
517	Wedgewood, Dark	
964	Seagreen, Light	
3727	Antique Mauve, Light	
3750	Antique Blue, Very Dark	
3760	Wedgewood, Medium	
3848	Teal Green, Medium	

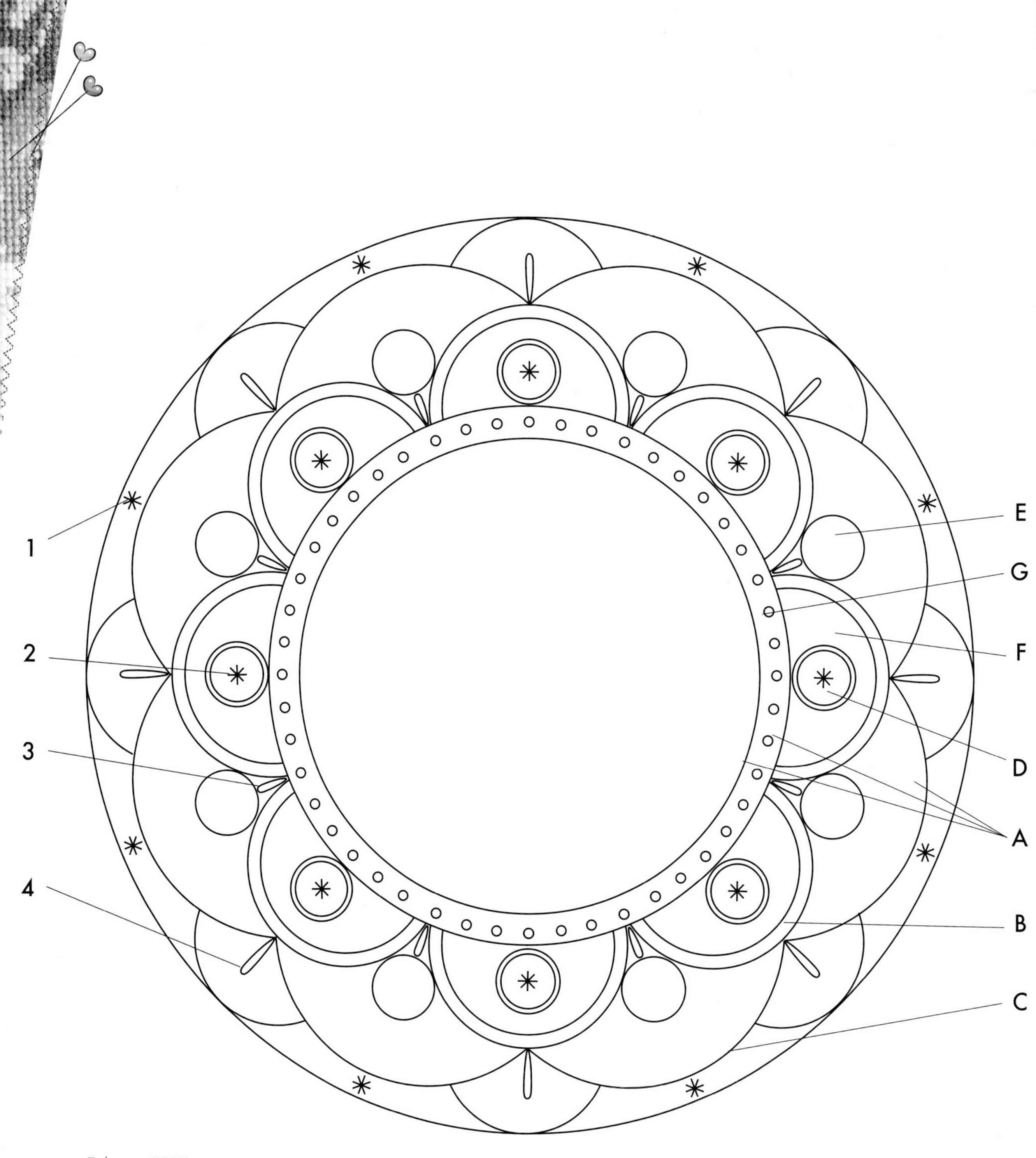

Enlarge 175%

Instructions

1 Begin by cutting your fabric square then **ironing** it, and **transfer** your design by whichever method you choose. Then choose the largest embroidery hoop you have or grab your frame and **stretch your fabric**, making sure your design is not warped.

2 Start your embroidery with the **3 green circles (A)** that form the embroidered structure of your frame, using the chain stitch with a triple thread of 3848. Make sure not to pull on your threads so as to avoid creating tension between the thread and the fabric.
Embroidering with 3 threads makes a notable difference in thread tension and you must train your hand to feel the fluidity of your gestures and adapt it to each type of embroidery.

3 Next embroider the **pink arches (B)** using the chain stitch with a triple thread of 3727.

4 Next embroider the **red arches (C)** using the chain stitch with a triple thread of 3750.

5 Now embroider the **light green circles (D)** using the chain stitch with a triple thread of 964, then the **navy blue circles (E)** using the chain stitch with a triple thread of 3650.

6 Next embroider the **orange arche (F)** using French knots with a triple thread of 352, making two twists around the needle, then embroider the **light green arches (that span the C arches)** using the same technique with 964.

7 Using the same technique with French knots, now embroider **1 light green circle in G** with 964 between the **2 green circles** that form the inside of the mirror frame. Then, still using French knots, embroider the **little pink circles** inside the D circles with a triple thread of 3727.

8 Next embroider the **stars (1)** above the red arches using the Rhodes (star) stitch, alternating between triple threads of 3760 and 3727.

9 Next embroider the **little teal stars (2)** inside the pink circles using the eyelet (star) stitch with a triple thread of 3760.

10 Lastly, embroider the **pompoms** using tuft couching. For the inner circle pompoms (3)use **bundles of 12 strands** folded in two, and for the outer circle pompoms (4), use **bundles of 24 strands** folded in two.

Congratulations, you have now completed the embroidery and can move on to assembling the mirror!

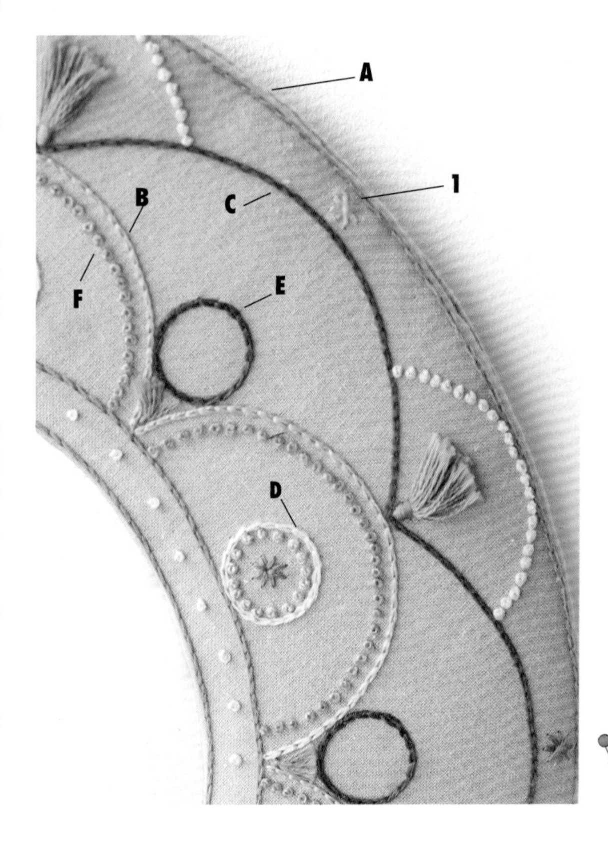

Assembling the mirror

1 Carefully cut out 3 circles of recycled cardboard and one of batting:

- one circle the size of the embroidery,
- another with the outer circumference matching your embroidery, and the inner circumference corresponding to your mirror
- and the third—which you will cut in both cardboard and batting—with an outer circumference matching the outer edge of your embroidery and an inner circumference matching the inner edge of the embroidery.

2 Take your first circle and lay it on a separate piece of your ground fabric. Cut a circle ½" (1cm) from the edge of your cardboard circle, then fold this extra fabric up over the cardboard all around the circumference. Glue it in place with strong glue.

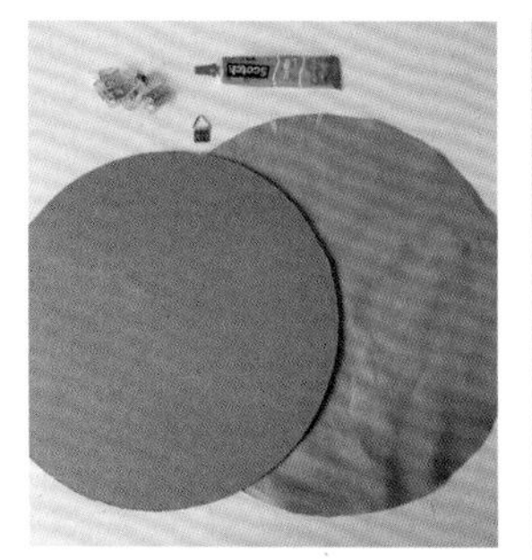

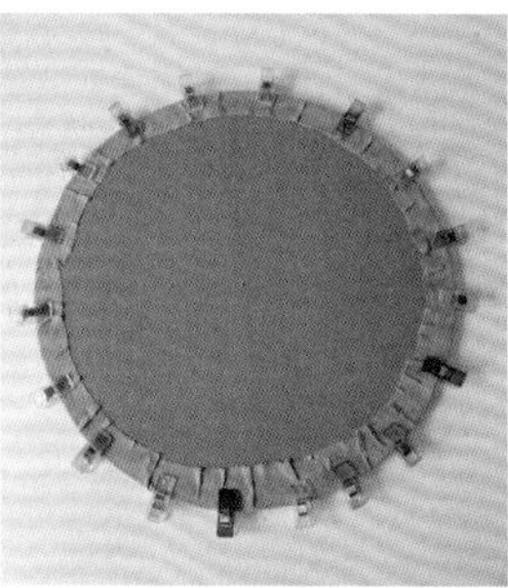

You can use clips or clothespins to hold your fabric in place while the glue dries. The fabric should be pulled tight so that the covered side is nice and smooth.

3 Grab your ring hanger and sew it to the side covered in fabric, where you would position a picture hanger. You can reinforce this by covering your stitches with some glue on the reverse side.

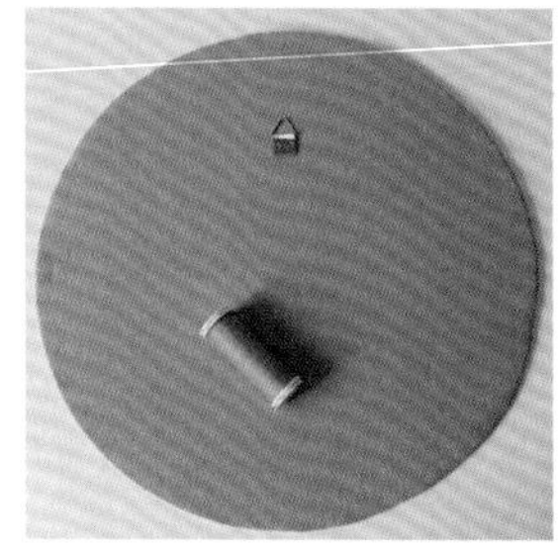

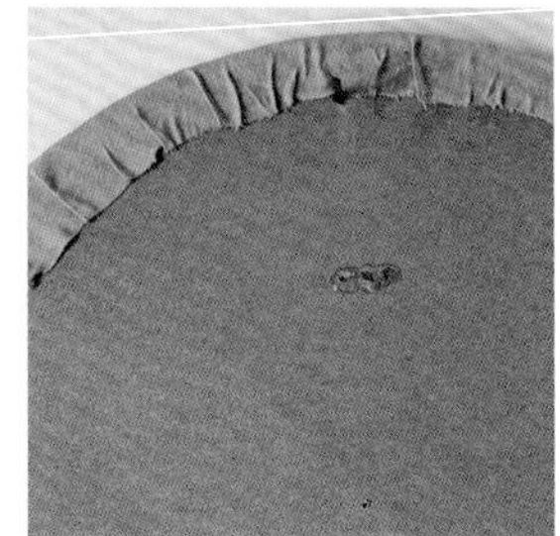

4 Next take your embroidery and cut 1" (2cm) from the outer and inner edges of the embroidery. Make little notches every ½" (1cm) around the inner edge of the embroidery.

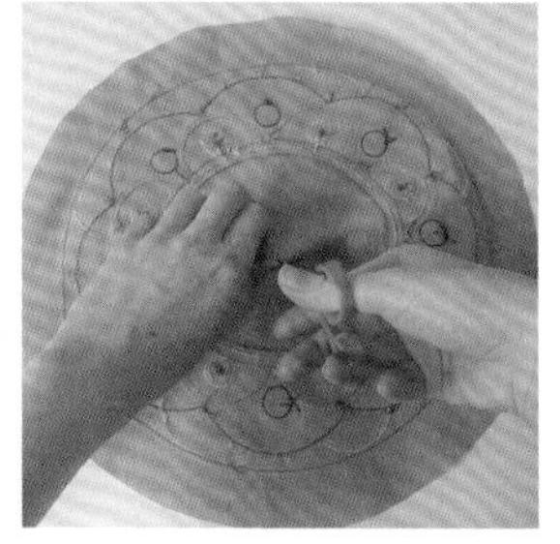

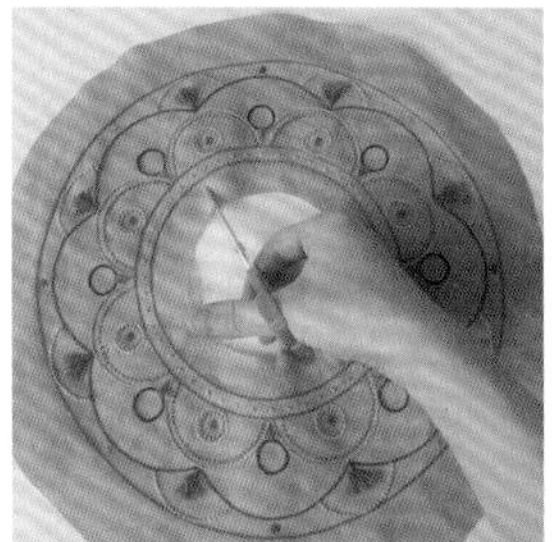

5 Glue your second and third cardboard circles together. Lay the embroidery on the batting, then place both on top of the two circles you have just assembled (the flat surface against the embroidery). We can now permanently assemble all the pieces together.

6 Using your clips or clothespins, position your embroidery so it matches the cardboard circles, making sure that the batting is well-positioned between the embroidery and the top circle. Once you're happy with the placement, turn it over and glue your fabric.

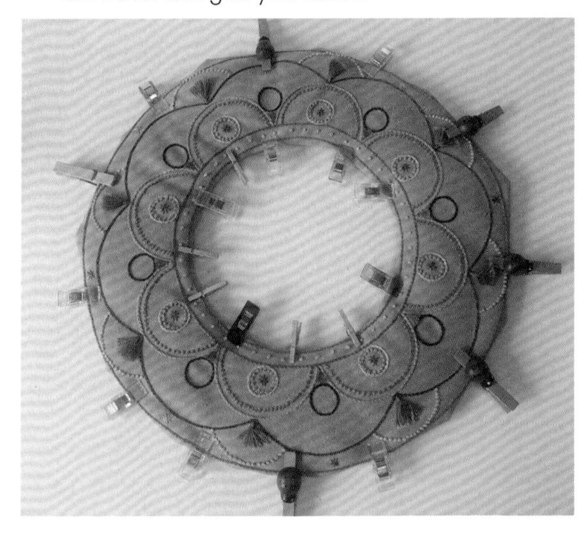

7 Using double-sided tape, stick your mirror in the middle of your first cardboard circle (on the side not covered with fabric), then spread glue over the rest of the cardboard not covered by the mirror.

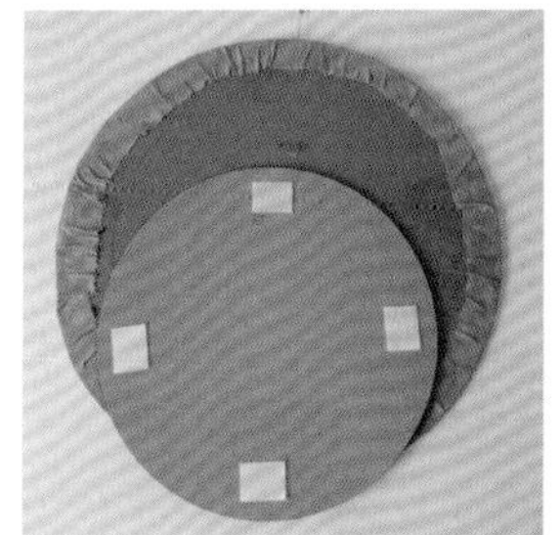

8 Glue the embroidery/cardboard component onto the cardboard with the mirror. Press together well, wait a few minutes, then, with a tiny invisible stitch, join the 2 pieces of fabric by sewing all around the circumference of the frame.

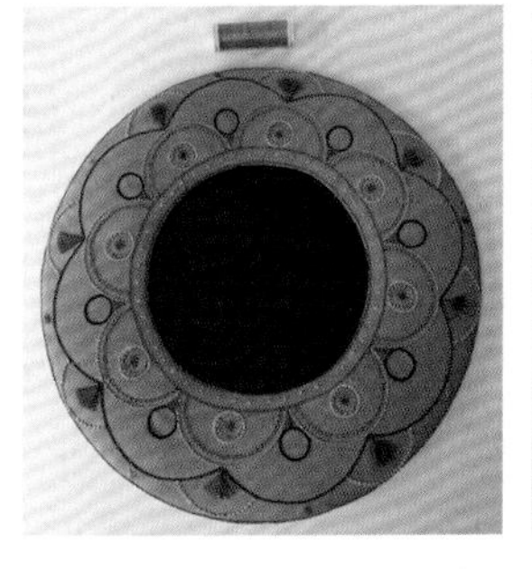

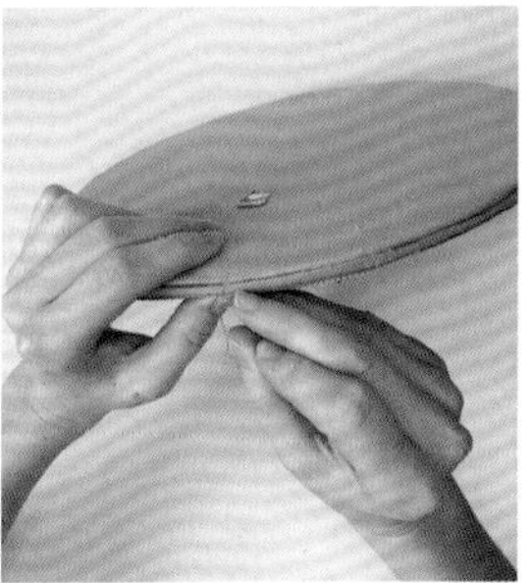

"Mirror, mirror, on the wall, who's the best embroiderer of all?"

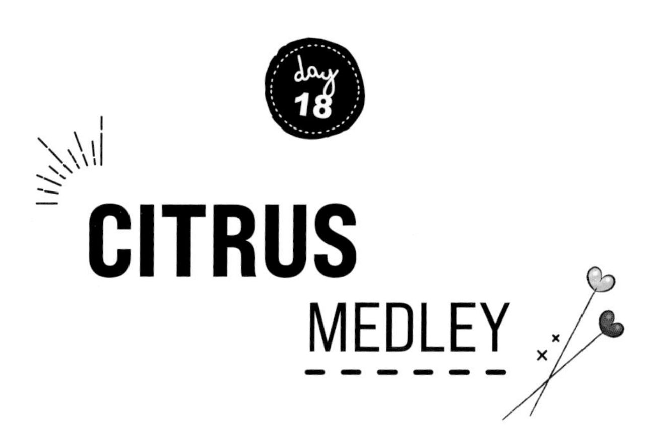

CITRUS MEDLEY

MASTER DIFFERENT TYPES OF BEADS AND RHINESTONES

Now let's take a look at a very exciting aspect of embroidery: embroidering with beads and rhinestones.

Beads, just like needles, have a **number** that corresponds to their size: the bigger the number, the smaller the bead.

There are several categories of beads: **seed beads** (classic round beads for embroidery), **tubes** or **bugles** (longer than they are wide), **charlottes** (round beads with a facet), **facetted** beads, **bicones**, and **novelty** beads (barrels, drops, funky beads, **semi-precious** beads, natural beads, wooden, glass, plastic beads, etc.). You can also find "color-lined" beads—clear beads with a different color on the inside.

The second material is that little miracle of light called the **rhinestone.** They come in synthetic crystal, glass, or resin and are facetted like precious stones. You can find **sew-on** rhinestones and **glue-on** rhinestones (hotfix rhinestones); sew-on rhinestones attach more securely. They come in all varieties: drops, navettes, chaton (round) rhinestones, as well as all sorts novelty shapes. The setting is generally gold or silver colored, and if the back is flat, they're called "flatback."

Now that you have a better understanding of these two materials, it's up to you to look around online, in craft stores and bead shops.

Keep your beads sorted by color in boxes or jam jars. While you're embroidering, you can put each type of bead in the container's lid so they're easy to grab and don't get mixed up.

A little challenge

Now that you're a bead and rhinestone expert, I've got a nice challenge for you: a project that is ideal for introducing beads because you don't need too much precision; you just have to listen to your intuition and have some fun.

First things first: Go have a nice little shopping trip.

But there are some rules to our game:

- You have three colors: **lemon yellow, orange**, and **green** (light and dark);
- with these three colors in mind, create an assortment of beads and rhinestones, taking inspiration from the project photos. You'll need to have **different sizes** and **shades** within each color category, and you'll need **rhinestones, facetted beads**, and **bi-cones** for the centers of the fruit. You will also need **very small bugles** as well as **seed beads** and/or **charlottes**.

Don't forget: the larger your materials, the quicker you will fill the space!

Materials

2 rectangles 8" × 10" (20 × 25cm) of dark blue gingham fabric • 1 rectangle 2" × 4" (5 × 10cm) of dark blue gingham fabric • 2 rectangles 8" × 10" (20 × 25cm) of light blue fabric • 1 zipper 10" (20cm) • Assortment of beads and rhinestones (see guidelines above) • Sewing thread: yellow, green, orange • DMC Six-Strand Embroidery Floss: 225 (shell pink, very light

Stitches

Scattered beads • Back-stitched beads • Lazy daisy

Enlarge 125%

Instructions

1 Begin by **embroidering the outlines** of your fruits using a back stitch with your **smallest beads**, you can mix your beads or divide your fruit embroidery in sections: for example, you can embroidery one half of a fruit with **bugles** and the other half with **seed beads**. Embroidering your fruits with the smallest beads allows you to achieve a very clear finish.

2 Once your outline is finished, take your erasable pen and **trace** on the fabric the (approximate) outline of your **sparkly fruit center**.

3 Following the outline you've embroidered and avoiding the center you've just traced, **fill your fruit line by line**, alternating bead type. Another rule: so that your lines maintain a nice curve, you need to make sure they all fit well together. For example, if you have a line with a series of small beads then a series of big ones, the next line should begin with a series of big beads followed by a series of small ones. This way, your embroidery will stay balanced.

4 When all you have left is the center, you can individually stitch a **jumble of facetted beads**, bicones, and rhinestones. To attach the rhinestones, simply stitch twice through the holes on the backing.

5 Embroider all the **leaf** outlines with your little green beads, then apply the same technique used to embroider the fruit, embroidering the interior of one leaf per fruit (you can follow the model).

6 Lastly, embroider all the **flowers** using lazy daisy stitches with a double thread of DMC 225.

Once your embroidery is finished, you can move on to assembling your clutch.

Assembling the clutch

1 Layer your batting, the embroidered rectangle (embroidered side inward), the zipper (right side against right side), and finally the lining rectangle. The zipper should be sandwiched between the two fabric rectangles.

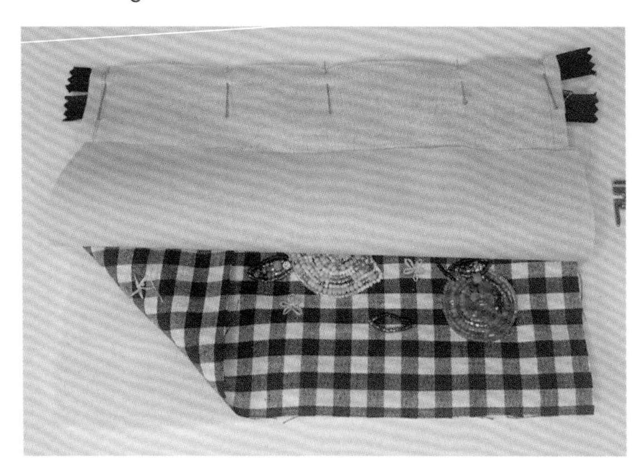

2 Use your sewing machine's zipper foot and begin sewing ½″ (1cm) from the edge. Then **sew** along the zipper using your zipper foot.

3 **Trim** the seams and cut out the extra batting.

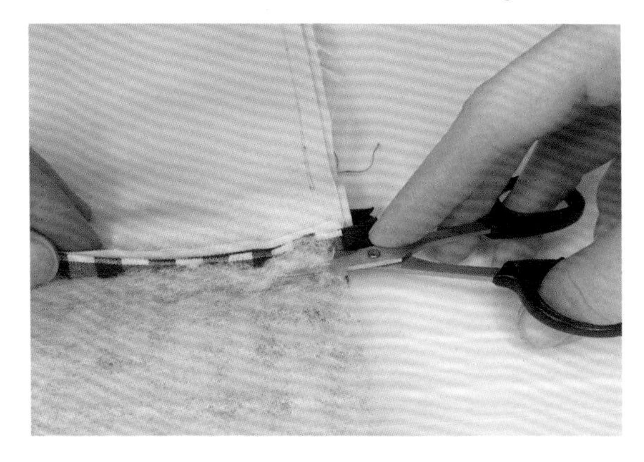

4 Turn your work right side out, choose a slightly longer stitch (7 stitches per inch or 3.5mm, for example), then **top stitch** very near the edge of the zipper, holding it with your hand to make sure it remains taut.

5 Repeat for the other side. Make sure the slider is on the inside of the clutch. If it gets in your way while you're sewing, lower the needle into the fabric, raise the presser foot, move the slider a little further along, lower the presser foot, and resume your sewing.

6 Now take your 2″ × 4″ (5 × 10cm) rectangle and fold it in half lengthwise right sides together. Sew along the long edge of the rectangle ½″ (1cm) from the edge and turn it right side out. Then fold it in half and pin as shown in the photo.

7 Next position your fabrics so that lining is against lining right sides together and so that your gingham rectangles—along with the batting rectangles—are against one another. You can now sew ½″ (1 cm) from the edge, making sure not to obstruct the zipper and leaving an opening (*see photo: between the two red pins*) so that you can turn your work right side out.

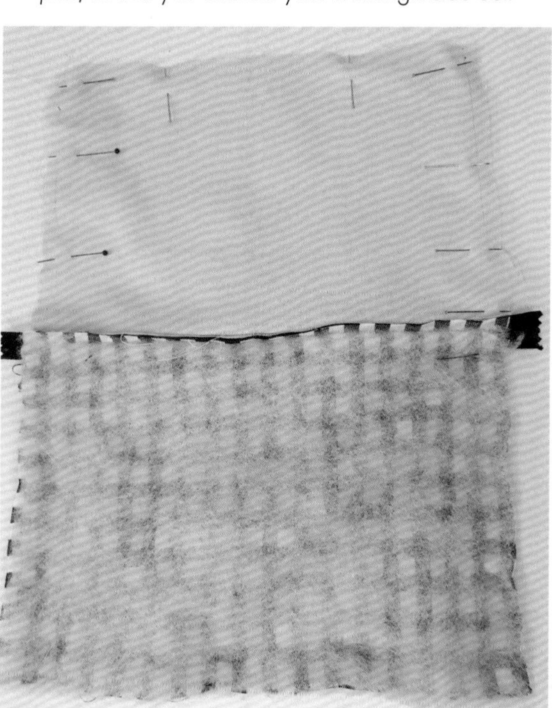

8 Turn your work right side out, **close the lining** using a small stitch as close to the edge as possible, then put the lining into the clutch. Finish with a quick iron for that final touch of perfection!!

You now have a sparkling clutch to make you stand out in a crowd!

THE DRAGONFLY'S FLIGHT

EMBROIDER WITH SEQUINS, CUT OUT YOUR EMBROIDERY, AND ATTACH IT TO A COMB

After beads, you've guessed it: sequins!
Sequins are little pierced discs with which you can embroider or sew.

This is a magnificent material that will allow you to create beautiful bejeweled embroidery. You can find them at any of the places you buy beads, so refer back to yesterday's project and don't forget to take another look at your Herbarium (Day 4) or your sampler (Day 3) to refresh your memory of the technique. Let's go!

GOOD TO KNOW

There are three categories of sequins: flat sequins, cup sequins—which, as the name would indicate, are shaped like cups—and novelty sequins, which come in all shapes. You can find sequins that are shiny or matte, transparent or opaque, iridescent, sparkly, made of plastic or metal; in short, anything you can imagine. They reflect the light and add life to your fabric.

Materials

A 10″ × 10″ square of silk organza • Some blue facetted beads • Some color-lined turquoise beads • 1 violet bead • Sequins: 5mm sequins (emerald green, gray blue, violet, pink, and gold), 1 gold cup sequin 4mm, 4mm sequins (blue, pink, and gold), 3mm sequins (pink and gold) • Sewing thread: pink and sea green

For assembly

Gold comb • Purple felt • Gold colored wire • Pliers

Stitches

Back-stitched beads • Beaded fringes • Scattered beads • Overlapping sequins • Beaded sequins

Instructions

1 Begin by tracing the outline of your dragonfly and flower on the organza. Leave an inch (a few centimeters) **between the two**.

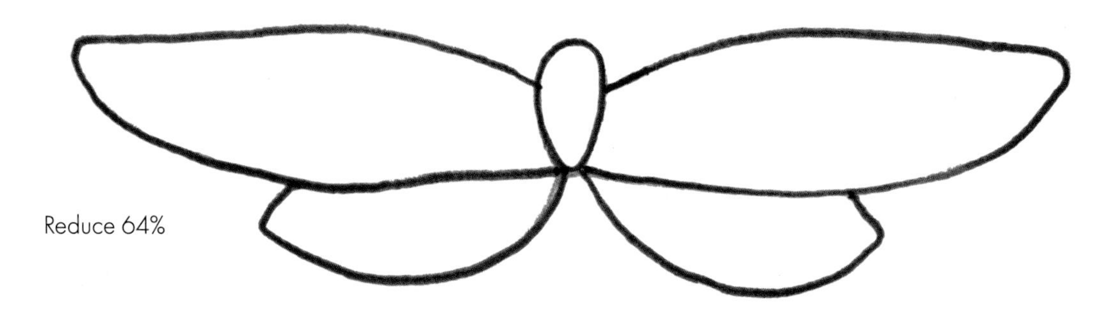

Reduce 64%

2 The dragonfly wings are entirely embroidered with overlapping sequins; alternate between two threads according to the color of your sequins. We're going to **start at the base of the upper wings** and progress upward. You can **embroider** both wings at the same time. To embroider these wings, we're going line by line, **always going from the outside in**. Additionally, we will embroider the sequins **from larger to smaller**, with a **gradation** of colors: green, blue, pink, and gold, adding a couple gold sequins here and there along the way.

- **For the first line**: 6 green sequins 5mm, 5 blue sequins 5mm, 3 blue sequins 4mm, 1 gold sequin 4mm, 2 pink sequins 4mm, 3 pink sequins 3mm, 1 gold sequin 3mm.

- **Second line**: 5 green sequins 5mm, 4 blue sequins 5mm, 1 gold sequin 4mm, 3 blue sequins 4mm, 1 gold sequin 4mm, 1 pink sequin 4mm, 3 pink sequins 3mm.
- **Third line**: 3 green sequins 5mm, 1 gold sequin 5mm, 4 blue sequins 5mm, 1 gold sequin 4mm, 1 blue sequin 4mm, 2 pink sequins 4mm, 1 pink sequin 3mm, 1 gold sequin 3mm, 1 pink sequin 3mm, 1 gold sequin 3mm.
- **Fourth line**: 3 green sequins 5mm, 1 gold sequin 5mm, 2 blue sequins 5mm, 1 gold sequin 4mm, 1 blue sequin 4mm, 1 pink sequin 4mm, 1 blue sequin 4mm, 1 gold sequin 3mm.

You've now finished the two upper wings, you can now move on to the lower wings. Again, we'll start with the bottom line before moving on to the top line.

3 For the lower wings, you will again embroider from the outside in.

- For the **first line**: 2 violet sequins 5mm, 2 green sequins 5mm, 1 violet sequin 5mm, 2 green sequins 5mm, 1 violet sequin 5mm.
- For the **second line**: embroider the entire line with 5mm green sequins.

4 Now, for the **body**, embroider all along the outline of the body 1 line of turquoise color-lined beads using a back stitch with the sea green thread. Fill the shape this creates with the same beads using the scattered beads technique (they don't need to be too tightly packed in together).

5 Cut a length of wire and thread your beads, alternating between 1 turquoise bead and 1 facetted blue bead.

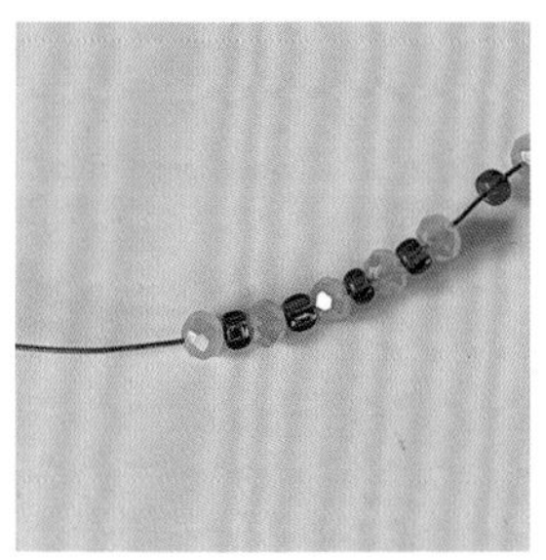

Once you've reached a length of **1½″ to 2″** (3 or 4cm), fold the wire and run it back through all the beads except the first one, using the beaded fringe technique.

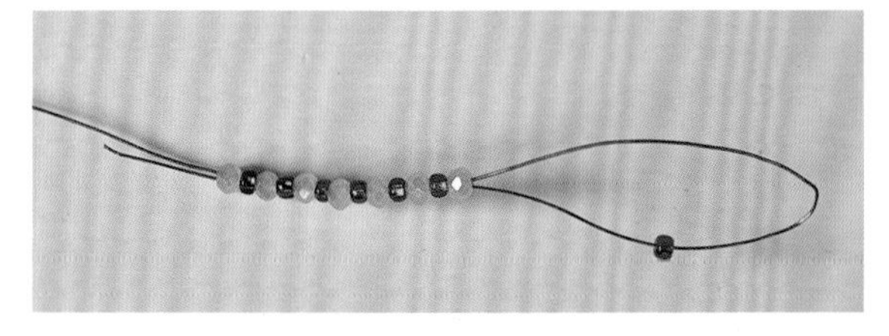

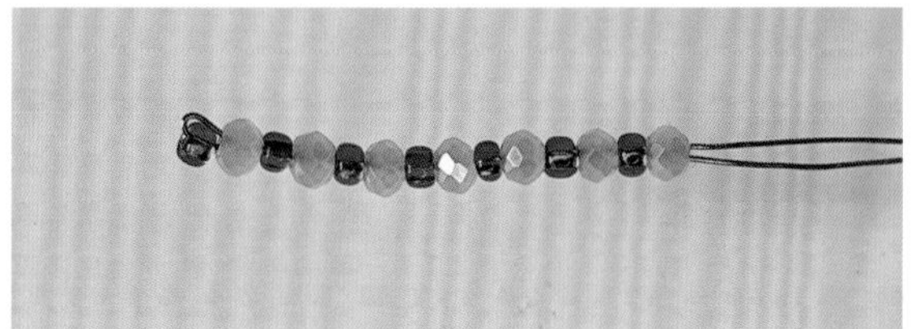

6 To make the flower, embroider petal by petal, following the outline of the design, from the outside in. You will have two types of petals that you will alternate between:

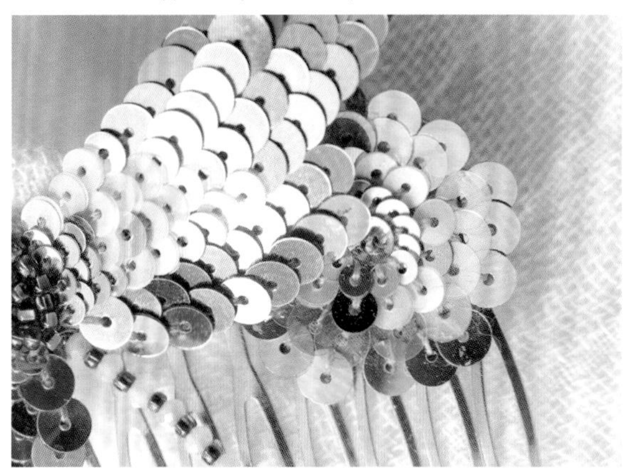

- Petal 1: 1 bright pink sequin 5mm, 1 see-through pink sequin 5mm, 1 iridescent pink sequin (or alternately gold) 4mm, 1 pink sequin (or alternately gold) 3mm. Repeat this line until you've covered the petal.
- Petal 2: 1 bright violet sequin 5mm, 1 see-through pink sequin 4mm, 1 iridescent pink sequin (or alternately gold) 4mm, 1 pink sequin (or alternately gold) 3mm.

Once your petals are finished, place one 4mm gold cup sequin held in place by one violet bead in the center.

Assembly

1 Dilute some white glue with water, and **apply it** with a paintbrush to the back of your embroidery, going about ¼" (5mm) beyond the outline of your design.

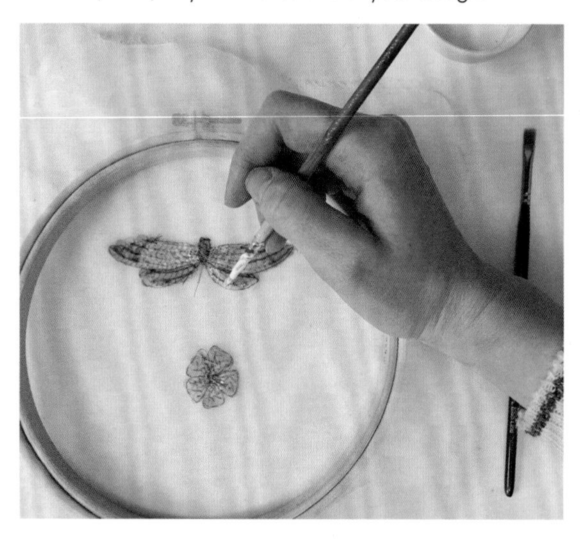

2 Once the glue has dried, **cut** around your embroidery about ¼" (5mm) from the edge and notch the curves. Fold the edges of the organza over and lightly press.

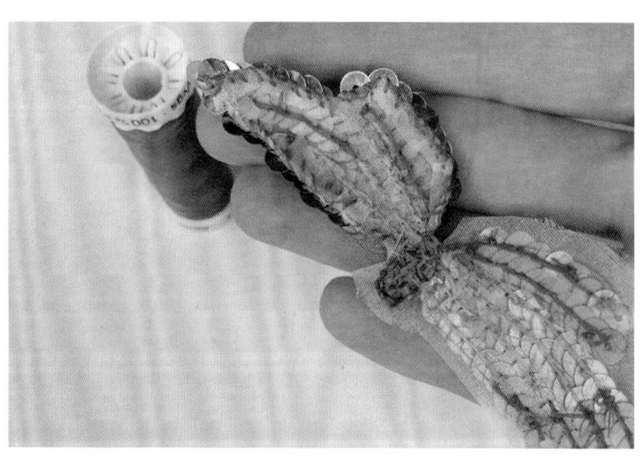

3 Grab your little beaded wire and create a small loop at the end, then secure it by twisting the wire several times around the loop.

Cut your wire. To finish, attach the loop to the body of your dragonfly so that the attachment is hidden.

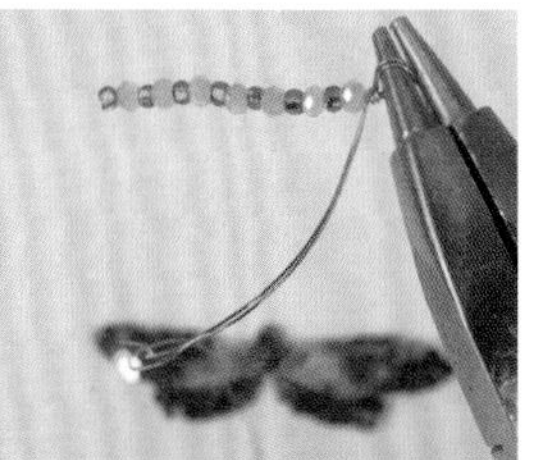

4 Cut the piece of felt in the shape of each embroidered piece,

then attach it to the back of your embroidered pieces using a small invisible stitch. Finally, attach your embroidery to your comb with a small stitch.

Slide the comb into your hair for a dazzling new do!

CELEBRATION NIGHT

MIX MEDIA: PAINTING, EMBROIDERY, AND DRIED FLOWERS!

For this, our last project, I wanted something that would be accessible to all but that would throw open the doors of your imagination. Mixing watercolors and embroidery helps you achieve great backdrops, immerses you in the design, and also saves you time (yes, painting can be faster than embroidery!), to create rich and diverse worlds. Glue a few dried flowers to your work, and you have an added touch of texture and life. Use this last embroidery lesson to celebrate yourself and appreciate the road you've traveled. So, for the last time, to the needles!

Materials

One 10" and one 12" (or larger) embroidery hoop • A palette of watercolors or ink • A 12" × 12" (30 × 30cm) square of natural cotton • DMC Six-Strand Embroidery Floss: 23, 309, 320, 564, 760, 761, 954, 992, 996, 3340, 3750, 3833, 3836, 3847 • Dried flowers • A tube of strong glue

Stitches

Running stitch • Chain stitch • Stem stitch • Fishbone stitch • Star stitch • Fly stitch • Lazy daisy • French knots • Bullion knots • Woven wheel stitch

DMC number	Color description	Substitution floss
23	Apple Blossom	
309	Rose, Dark	
320	Pistachio Green, Medium	
564	Jade, Very Light	
760	Salmon	
761	Salmon, Light	
954	Nile Green	
992	Aquamarine, Light	
996	Electric Blue, Medium	
3340	Apricot, Medium	
3750	Antique Blue, Very Dark	
3833	Raspberry, Light	
3836	Grape, Light	
3847	Teal Green, Dark	

Instructions

1 Take your larger embroidery hoop or frame and stretch your fabric. Once the fabric is tight, transfer the outline of the design. Remove the fabric from the hoop.

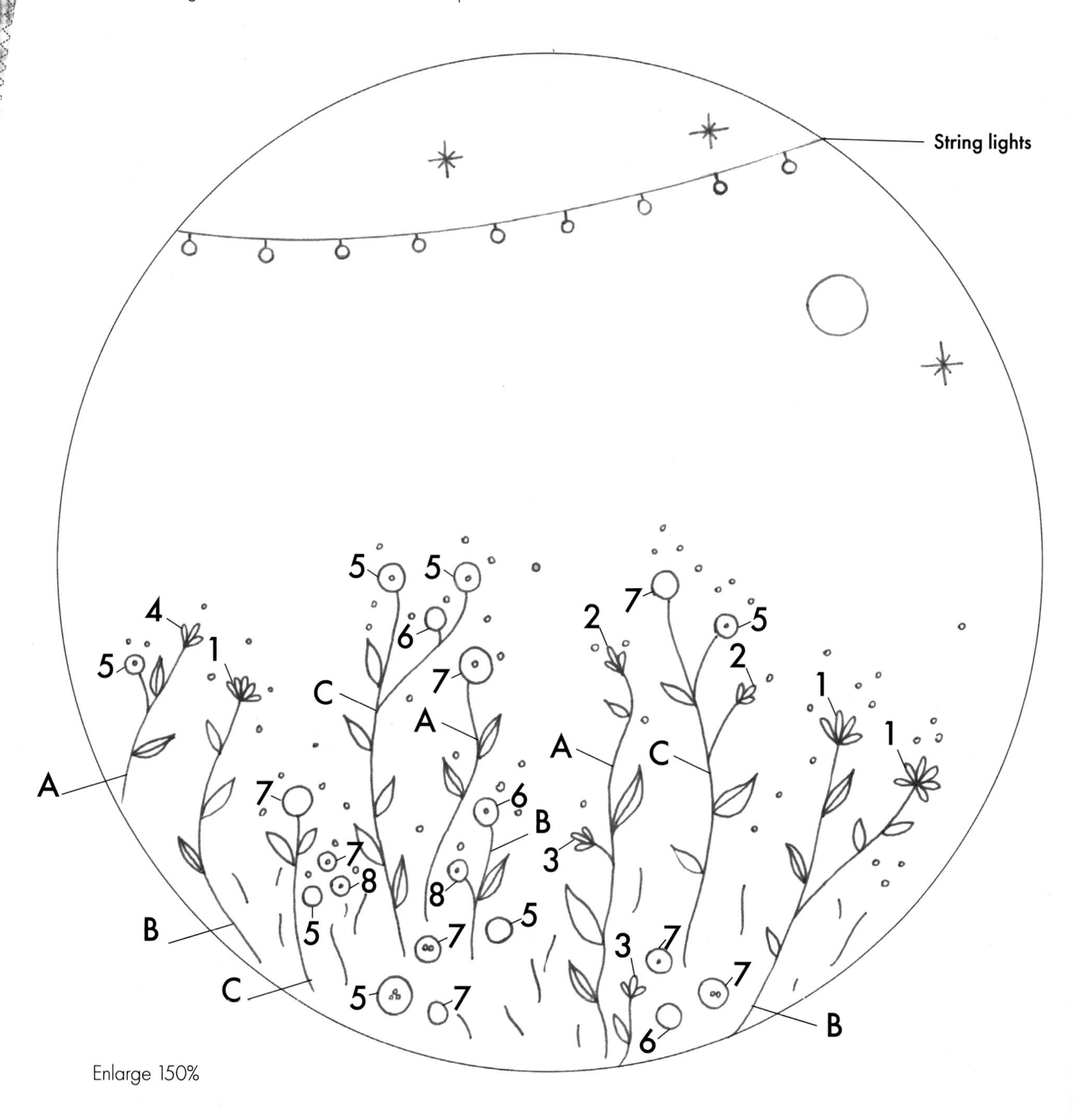

Enlarge 150%

2 Get a large glass of water and your watercolors and settle in. Start by **moistening your fabric**.

3 Then, following the steps shown in the photos, **add the colors** to your fabric. You can go beyond the circle, it doesn't matter. If you find that your color is too intense, you can dilute it by simply adding water to your fabric with your brush, and if your color is too weak, you can add more pigment. It's very easy to adjust, to correct; you'll see, it's very easy!

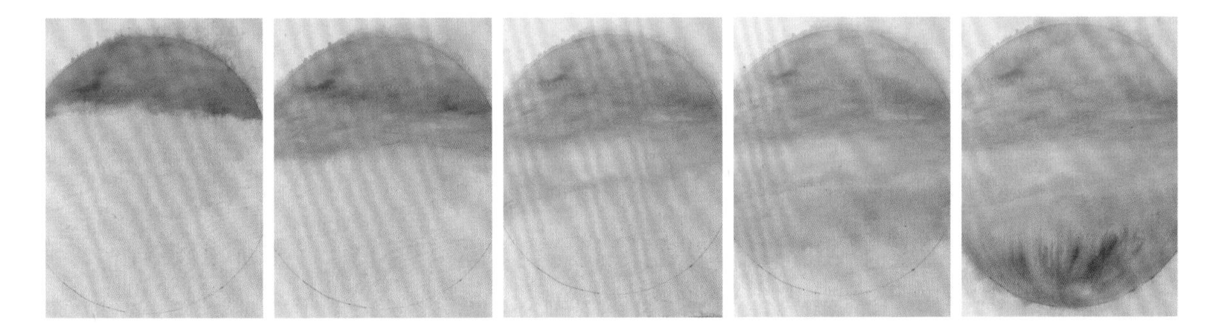

4 Once your watercolors have dried, **transfer your design** to the fabric. Take some white watercolor or ink and, adding as little water as possible, draw the two stars and the moon, then wait for it to dry again.

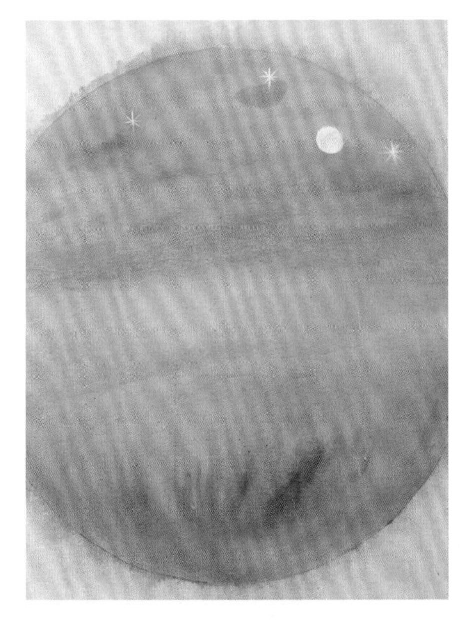

5 Begin by **embroidering** the string lights. The **wire** is made using the chain stitch with a single strand of 3750, and the **little connections between the wire and the lights** are made using a running stitch with a double thread of 3750. Last, the **bulbs** are made using the Rhodes (star) stitch with a double thread, alternating between 4 colors, in order: 3340, 3833, 996, and 954.

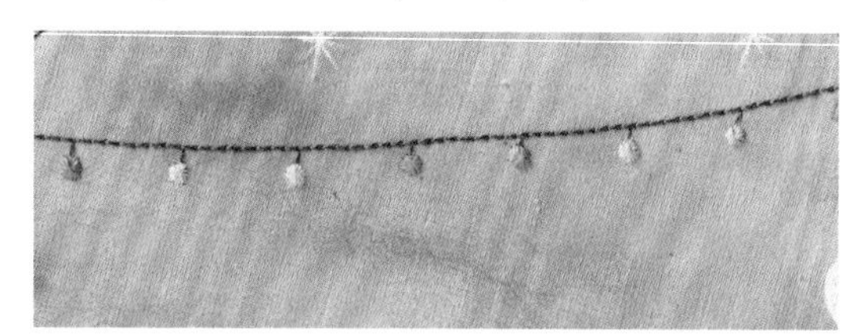

6 You can now embroider the **stalks** using the stem stitch with a double thread.

Stalk As: 992; Stalk Bs: 3847; Stalk Cs: 320.

Once you've finished the stalks, embroider the scattered blades of grass using the same technique, alternating between these 3 colors.

7 Next embroider the flowers:

the **flowers with looped petals** using the lazy daisy stitch with a double thread,

the **circular flowers** with a little ball in the middle using the **woven wheel stitch and a French knot** in the middle with a double thread (2 twists around the needle),

the **circular flowers without a little ball** in the center using bullion knots with a double thread.

For the colors:
flower 1s: 309,

flower 2s: 761 for the outer petals and 760 for the inner petal,

flower 3s: 760 for the outer petals and 761 for the inner petal,

flower 4s: 761 for the outer petals and 3836 for the inner petal,

flower 5s: 3836 for the flowers, and 761 for the French knots at the center,

flower 6s: 309 for the flowers, and 3836 for the French knots at the center,

flower 7s: 761 for the flowers, and 3836 for the French knots at the center,

flower 8s: 760 for the flowers, and 761 for the French knots at the center.

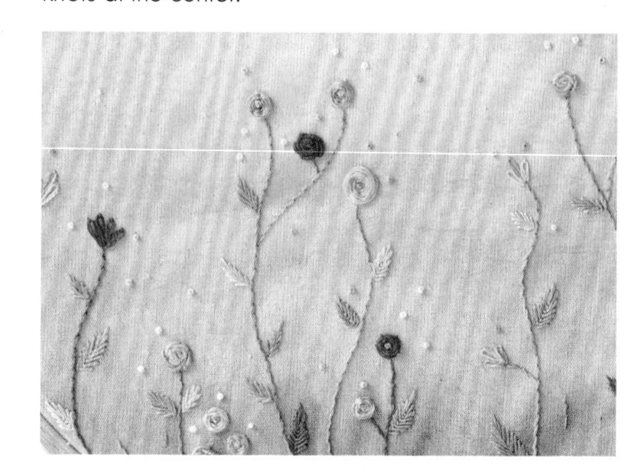

8 Last, you can embroider all the little **scattered dots** using French knots with a double thread (2 twists around the needle) randomly with colors 23, 761, and 3836.

9 Position your work in the 10″ (26cm) embroidery hoop and, using the strong glue, stick the **dried flowers** onto the outer circle of your hoop.

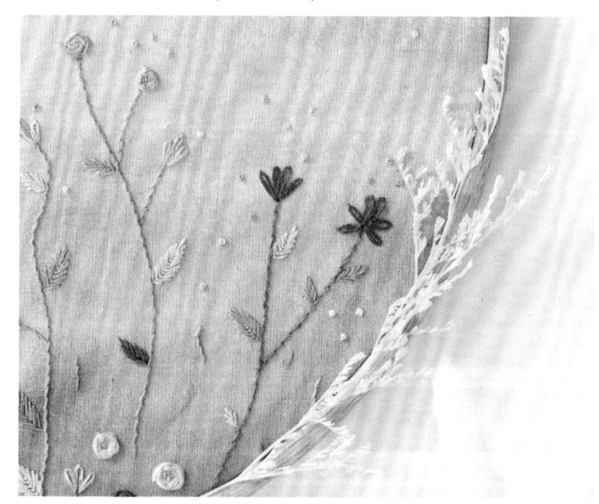

You've completed the last project in this book, I hope you enjoyed yourself! Come back tomorrow for the last lesson—last, but definitely not least.

IT'S your TURN

CREATE YOUR OWN PROJECTS

Now it's your turn to scribble away in notebooks, jot down ideas, take pictures of what inspires you. You have everything you need to create some magnificent embroidery, so let's talk a little about the creative process for making your own designs.

Start by getting yourself a nice notebook (preferably full-sized), in which you will glue, tape, and draw all sorts of images, color schemes, ideas, paintings, song lyrics and movie quotes... Fill it with life and color. Not everything has to be beautiful but it should bring you pleasure and make you want to open up that notebook.

The second thing you can do, if the idea speaks to you, is to create moodboards* on Pinterest. You can collect images (photos, drawings, paintings, etc.) according to your interests and what you find, or even create boards with a thematic idea in head and cultivate that idea with as many inspiring photos as you like.

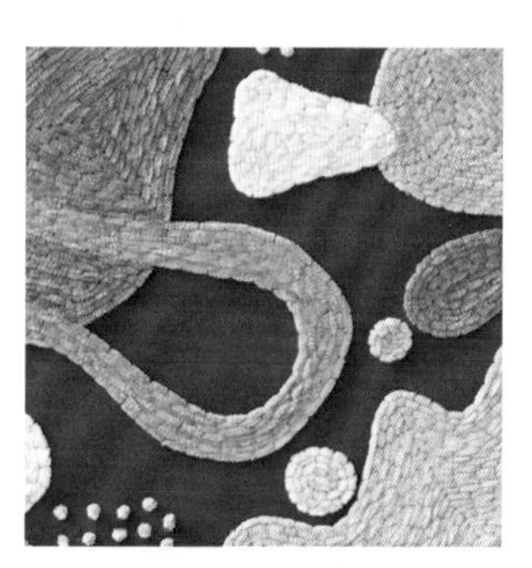

Come up with a theme

As you go about your day, you hear a phrase or maybe a word that resonates like a desire to embroider, gazing at the clouds, listening to music, looking out at the ocean, or deep in thought, settled at your desk, with a cup of tea, you had an idea...

Ideas, sometimes you'll have ten in a day, and then other times you might feel paralyzed before the blank page. At those moments, don't hesitate to get out, get a fresh perspective at an arts and crafts store, a hobby shop, a museum, a movie theater, or even just out for a walk. And, of course, there's always time to do a little browsing on Instagram or Pinterest to find a bit of inspiration.

You can also choose your theme based on what you want to give as a gift, what you want to carry or wear, or an object you want for your home.

Now's the time to crack that notebook wide open, think about what makes you smile, what colors you like, to explore all available avenues of every nascent idea that passes through your head.

Go a little further....

Once you have hold of a marvelous idea, which can be simple or complicated, start a fresh page in your notebook and analyze it, write down any associated ideas, definitions, intuitions. Make some little sketches and finally eliminate whatever you don't like, and allow yourself to wander a bit.

This page is just for you: it's for smoothing out the rough patches and finding a central axis for your theme. Naturally there's more than one way to develop your theme, and if you like, you can explore different paths at the same time.

The little project preliminaries

Once your theme is set in place, make an image search for reference (stylistic, anatomical, compositional, etc.) that will help in your design and in deepening your initial intuitions.

Grab a pencil, an eraser, and some colored pencils and create a new page with different drafts of your composition. The design doesn't need to be polished or beautiful right away, let your instincts run free, you can adjust lines later. Identify the shapes you like, imagine an overall composition. When these steps are done, you can refine your design.

Give substance to your idea

Choosing your textures and materials can also be a great source of inspiration. Don't hesitate to lay them all out in front of you and play with them to create diverse and varied compositions until you find the combination that speaks to you.

You should also consult your herbarium (or sampler) for inspiration when it comes to the textures, thicknesses, and designs offered by the different embroidery stitches.

You can discover wonderful variations of the stitches you've already learned on Pinterest, YouTube, and on blogs.

Choose a color palette

Have fun choosing your colors. You have infinite combinations available to you. Don't be afraid to use contrasting colors or, on the other end of the spectrum, to play with several shades of the same color.

You can determine your colors right on your design, which will save you time when you get to the embroidery stage. But you can also decide on your colors as you embroider. It's a longer process, but it allows for a more feelings-based approach. To help you, you can choose a variety of skeins that go well together and stick to this collection throughout your project.

Take a step back

It is sometimes necessary to step away for a bit to maintain objectivity toward your work. I recommend taking a little break: go for a walk, sleep on it, or visit some friends. You'll probably see things more clearly and more confidently when it comes to what you like and don't like in your composition. Make adjustments (or don't), and get back into it!

To help you determine if a composition is balanced and works, it can be quite useful to take a picture and look at it in the mirror.

And voila! You're done! You now have all the tools you need to be independent in your embroidery. You've completely mastered the technique and the world of creation lays before you. Free your imagination and jump right in.

Trust yourself and above all, **have fun!**

*Moodboard: A board of trends or inspiration that helps you define the aesthetic backbone of a project.